American University
Washington, DC

Written by Alanna Schubach

Edited by Adam Burns, Kristen Burns, and Jon Skindzier

Layout by Meghan Dowdell

*Additional contributions by Omid Gohari,
Christina Koshzow, Chris Mason, Joey Rahimi,
and Luke Skurman*

ISBN # 1-4274-0012-1
ISSN # 1551-9422
© Copyright 2006 College Prowler
All Rights Reserved
Printed in the U.S.A.
www.collegeprowler.com

Last updated 5/13/06

Special Thanks To: Babs Carryer, Andy Hannah, LaunchCyte, Tim O'Brien, Bob Sehlinger, Thomas Emerson, Andrew Skurman, Barbara Skurman, Bert Mann, Dave Lehman, Daniel Fayock, Chris Babyak, The Donald H. Jones Center for Entrepreneurship, Terry Slease, Jerry McGinnis, Bill Ecenberger, Idie McGinty, Kyle Russell, Jacque Zaremba, Larry Winderbaum, Roland Allen, Jon Reider, Team Evankovich, Lauren Varacalli, Abu Noaman, Mark Exler, Daniel Steinmeyer, Jared Cohon, Gabriela Oates, David Koegler, and Glen Meakem.

Bounce-Back Team: Lindsey McDaniel, Greg Kellner, and Amanda Thickpenny.

College Prowler®
5001 Baum Blvd.
Suite 750
Pittsburgh, PA 15213

Phone: 1-800-290-2682
Fax: 1-800-772-4972
E-Mail: info@collegeprowler.com
Web Site: www.collegeprowler.com

Welcome to College Prowler®

During the writing of College Prowler's guidebooks, we felt it was critical that our content was unbiased and unaffiliated with any college or university. We think it's important that our readers get honest information and a realistic impression of the student opinions on any campus—that's why if any aspect of a particular school is terrible, we (unlike a campus brochure) intend to publish it. While we do keep an eye out for the occasional extremist—the cheerleader or the cynic—we take pride in letting the students tell it like it is. We strive to create a book that's as representative as possible of each particular campus. Our books cover both the good and the bad, and whether the survey responses point to recurring trends or a variation in opinion, these sentiments are directly and proportionally expressed through our guides.

College Prowler guidebooks are in the hands of students throughout the entire process of their creation. Because you can't make student-written guides without the students, we have students at each campus who help write, randomly survey their peers, edit, layout, and perform accuracy checks on every book that we publish. From the very beginning, student writers gather the most up-to-date stats, facts, and inside information on their colleges. They fill each section with student quotes and summarize the findings in editorial reviews. In addition, each school receives a collection of letter grades (A through F) that reflect student opinion and help to represent contentment, prominence, or satisfaction for each of our 20 specific categories. Just as in grade school, the higher the mark the more content, more prominent, or more satisfied the students are with the particular category.

Once a book is written, additional students serve as editors and check for accuracy even more extensively. Our bounce-back team—a group of randomly selected students who have no involvement with the project—are asked to read over the material in order to help ensure that the book accurately expresses every aspect of the university and its students. This same process is applied to the 200-plus schools College Prowler currently covers. Each book is the result of endless student contributions, hundreds of pages of research and writing, and countless hours of hard work. All of this has led to the creation of a student information network that stretches across the nation to every school that we cover. It's no easy accomplishment, but it's the reason that our guides are such a great resource.

When reading our books and looking at our grades, keep in mind that every college is different and that the students who make up each school are not uniform—as a result, it is important to assess schools on a case-by-case basis. Because it's impossible to summarize an entire school with a single number or description, each book provides a dialogue, not a decision, that's made up of 20 different topics and hundreds of student quotes. In the end, we hope that this guide will serve as a valuable tool in your college selection process. Enjoy!

OMID GOHARI ◯ CHRISTINA KOSHZOW ◯ CHRIS MASON ◯ JOEY RAHIMI ◯ LUKE SKURMAN ◯
The College Prowler Team

Table of Contents

Introduction from the Author

My choice to attend American University was somewhat random. I knew I wanted to live in a city and attend a school that offered strong journalism programs. I applied to six schools, was accepted to four, and found that American was the only one I could afford due to a scholarship package I was offered. At the time, I wasn't exactly ready to burst into song about it—when I told people where I was going, some had never even heard of AU. It all seemed very arbitrary, and I wondered if I was making a huge mistake.

Well, I can now say that some things truly do happen for a reason. American University and I are a great match, and I believe that many others will have similar experiences if they choose to attend AU. The school is diverse and ambitious, located in one of the most powerful and exciting cities in the world. There is something for everyone here, whether their interests are politics, history, culture, the arts, or nightlife. It may be overwhelming at first, but any adjustments are well worth the rewards of exposing yourself to such an unbelievable place.

In the '80s, American was known primarily as a party school, which goes to show how dramatically it has changed over the past two decades. Now the University attracts individuals from around the world who are interested in a wide variety of subjects. AU is bent on helping students grow into independent, intellectual people with strong foundations of knowledge upon which to build illustrious careers. The school is quickly growing in popularity and overall stature—and deservedly so. Now is an exciting time to attend American University, and to study among your ambitious, open-minded peers. Are you ready?

Alanna Schubach, Author
American University

By the Numbers

General Information

American University
4400 Massachusetts Ave.
Washington, DC 20016

Control:
Private

Academic Calendar:
Semester

Religious Affiliation:
Methodist

Founded:
1893

Web Site:
www.american.edu

Main Phone:
(202) 885-1000

Admissions Phone:
(202) 885-6000

Student Body

**Full-Time
Undergraduates:**
5,504

**Part-Time
Undergraduates:**
307

**Total Male
Undergraduates:**
2,231

**Total Female
Undergraduates:**
3,580

Admissions

Overall Acceptance Rate:
53%

Early Decision Acceptance Rate:
60%

Total Applicants:
12,198

Total Acceptances:
6,494

Freshman Enrollment:
1,209

Yield (% of admitted students who actually enroll):
19%

Regular Decision Deadline:
January 15

Regular Decision Notification:
April 1

Early Decision Available?
Yes

Early Decision Deadline:
November 15

Early Decision Notification:
December 31

Early Action Available?
No

Must-Reply-By Date:
May 1

Transfer Applications Received:
1,463

Transfer Applicants Accepted:
950

Transfer Students Enrolled:
415

Transfer Application Acceptance Rate:
65%

Common Application Accepted?
Yes

Supplemental Forms?
No

Admissions E-Mail:
afa@american.edu

Admissions Web Site:
http://admissions.american.edu

SAT I or ACT Required?
Either

SAT I Range (25th–75th Percentile):
1150–1350

SAT I Verbal Range (25th–75th Percentile):
580–690

SAT I Math Range (25th–75th Percentile):
570–660

First-Year Students Submitting SAT Scores:
95%

→

**Top 10% of High
School Class:**
44%

Application Fee:
$45

Freshman Retention Rate:
87%

Financial Information

Full-Time Tuition:
$28,019

Room and Board:
$10,700

Books and Supplies:
$600

**Average Need-Based
Financial Aid Package
(including loans, work-study,
grants, and other sources):**
$25,846

**Students Who Applied
for Financial Aid:**
59%

Students Who Received Aid:
47%

Financial Aid Forms Deadline:
February 15

Financial Aid Phone:
(202) 885-6100

Financial Aid E-Mail:
afa@american.edu

Financial Aid Web Site:
*http://admissions.
american.edu*

Academics

The Lowdown On...
Academics

Degrees Awarded:
Associate
Bachelor
Master
Doctorate

Undergraduate Schools:
College of Arts and Sciences
Kogod School of Business
School of Communication
School of International Service
School of Public Affairs
Washington College of Law

Most Popular Majors:
19% International Relations and Affairs

18% Business/Commerce

9% Communication and Speech Related Studies

9% Political Science and Government

7% Criminal Justice/Safety Studies

Full-Time Faculty:
490

Faculty with Terminal Degree:
96%

Student-to-Faculty Ratio:
15:1

Average Course Load:
12–17 credits

Graduation Rates:
Four-Year: 65%
Five-Year: 71%
Six-Year: 73%

Special Degree Options

ROTC, accelerated study, cooperative education, double major, student-designed major, teacher certification, Washington semester (for students from other universities), weekend college

AP Test Score Requirements

Credit for scores of 4 and 5

IB Test Score Requirements

Higher level tests for grades of 4 or higher

Did You Know?

The most highly-populated school is the **College of Arts and Sciences**.

Students began the Web site *www.benladner.com* in reaction to their former President, Ben Ladner, being found guilty of using University money for his own personal and travel expenses.

AU is a member of the **Consortium of Universities of the Washington Metropolitan Area**, allowing students to enroll in courses offered by other member institutions and students at other member institutions to enroll in courses at AU.

Sample Academic Clubs

Alpha Lambda Delta (honors fraternity), German Club, and the Society of Professional Journalists

Best Places to Study

Dorm formal lounges, the library, and the quad

Students Speak Out On...
Academics

{ **"Teachers vary. Some you will love; some you will hate. The great thing about DC is that you have teachers who also do other stuff while teaching, like being ambassadors to other countries."**

Q **"For the most part, my professors were great**. I was in the School of Public Affairs (SPA), and my SPA professors had great experience and knowledge. AU has a lot of adjunct professors, which means they work full time somewhere else (often in government positions) and then come to AU to teach one class each semester. I had professors who worked at the EPA, Department of Justice, and DC Court of Appeals. It adds such a good non-academic perspective."

Q "My classes were all small. My largest was a 60-person biology lecture; **my smallest class had seven**. The average was probably 12 students, so there was a lot of personal attention, and I always felt free to go to my professors' office hours for help."

Q "We have great professors here. Some can be boring, but most are pretty good, and **if you look and ask around, you will find out who the great ones are**. There are some that just blow your mind."

Q "The academics are not as impressive as you would think. **AU often tries to hire professors for their names rather than for their quality**. But opportunities in the city make up for shortfalls in the faculty. There are lots of good professors. Nonetheless, you just have to search for some of them."

Q "The teachers in the Kogod School of Business are great, as are the International Service professors and those in the School of Public Affairs. Many of them are fabulously connected to their industries, which can result in terrific internships. For the School of Communication, I would say it's hit or miss. **Many of them were, or are, good reporters, but they have difficulty teaching it**. Then again, you either have it or you don't, more often than not—you can't teach someone to smell news."

Q "**It all depends on your learning style and field that you're going to be studying**. If you have a major like history, the teachers are mainly lecturing the whole time. Education, on the other hand, is very hands-on; business is a mixture of both."

Q "The biggest classes we have are Micro and Macroeconomics. They can have up to 300 students, but the truth is that most classes don't exceed 30. **The teachers, for the most part, are very good**."

Q "Like any college, you have your good, and you have your bad. I really like my professors in the School of Public Affairs, but the math department is not so good. A lot of them have written books, or know prominent people, so they're really interesting to listen to. **All of them have been great when it comes to getting extra help**."

Q "Teachers are mostly good. The political and international teachers are the best. Law and business professors are probably runners up. **Most of my classes have about 20–30 students in them**, but every now and then, I get classes that are as small as 10 or as big as 200 students."

Q "The teachers, for the most part, are great. You have your bad apples everywhere, but basically one of the advantages of a small school is that **they are very personal and approachable** and very anxious to see you do well."

Q "**For some reason, AU has some of the best faculty members in the United States**. I've been exceedingly satisfied with 90 percent of the faculty I've had here. Most of the resident faculty have doctorates while those who are adjunct (meaning they have another job outside of teaching), have really great backgrounds, and have worked all over the map in top positions."

Q "I've had a few excellent professors, but **there are some dreadful ones as well**, some which are sadly unavoidable through general education classes."

Q "General education classes can be awesome, eye opening, or just the opposite. **Classes in my major and minors I've found to be very interesting**."

The College Prowler Take On...
Academics

Professors at American University tend to be experts in their fields, and many are involved with the government. Their diversity reflects the school's varied curriculum, and many agree that politics and business are the strongest areas of study. AU's location contributes greatly to students' learning experiences by providing hands-on opportunities, especially to international service, political science, and communications majors.

Most classes are small, and though there are a few professors who are bad apples, it doesn't ruin the overall academics of AU. Despite being a small school, AU has a great drawing power for well-known and respected faculty members. Don't be surprised to see professors being interviewed or called in for their expert opinions on the news. Students find DC to be an exciting and eye-opening city, and the school's classes reflect that.

The College Prowler® Grade on
Academics: A-

A high Academics grade generally indicates that professors are knowledgeable, accessible, and genuinely interested in their students' welfare. Other determining factors include class size, how well professors communicate, and whether or not classes are engaging.

Local Atmosphere

The Lowdown On...
Local Atmosphere

Region:
Mid Atlantic

City, State:
Washington, DC

Setting:
Major city

Distance from Baltimore:
1 hour

Distance from Philadelphia:
3 hours

Distance from New York:
4 hours

Points of Interest:
Adams Morgan
Alexandria
Dupont Circle
Georgetown
U Street

→

Closest Shopping Malls or Plazas:
Crystal City
Montgomery Mall
Tyson's Corner

Major Sports Teams:
Capitals (hockey)
Redskins (football)
Senators (baseball)
Wizards (basketball)

Closest Movie Theaters:
AMC Mazza Gallerie 7
5300 Wisconsin Ave. NW
Washington, DC
(202) 537-9553

(Movie Theaters, continued)
AMC Theatres
50 Massachusetts Ave.
Friendship Heights
(703) 998-4262

AMC Theatres
3426 Connecticut Ave.
Cleveland Park
(202) 966-5400

Avalon Theatre
5612 Connecticut Ave. NW
Washington, DC
(202) 966-6000

City Web Sites
www.dc.gov

Did You Know?

5 Fun Facts about Washington:

- It's **built on a swamp**.
- No buildings are allowed to be built higher than the **Washington Monument**.
- The **first election** in which residents legally participated was held in 1964.
- **DC itself is perfectly square**, and measures 15 miles on each edge.
- It's **divided into quadrants** (NE, NW, SE, SW), each with a distinct flavor.

Famous People from Wahington DC:

Tori Amos (Grammy-winning singer)

Alyson Hannigan (Actress—*American Pie*, *American Pie II*, *How I Met Your Mother*)

Goldie Hawn (Established actress, Kate Hudson's mom)

Marvin Gaye (Famous R&B singer)

Edward Norton (Actor—*Fight Club*, *Rounders*)

Local Slang:

No specific slang; DC is very much composed of residents native to other states, both northern and southern, so there's a wide range of speech patterns here.

Students Speak Out On...
Local Atmosphere

"In general, I was always told to stay away from Southeast DC. There are neighborhoods that don't seem safe, but which neighborhoods they are change over time. Visit all of the monuments: the Mall, Haines Point, and Old Town Alexandria."

Q "**This is DC—there's never a lack of things to do**. There are other major universities in town, like Georgetown, George Washington, and Howard University. George Mason, UMD, and UVA are not that far away."

Q "American is in a pretty residential area, but **it only takes about 20 minutes to get into the heart of DC**, where you will find GW. It takes about 15 minutes to get to Georgetown."

Q "DC is great. **It's a small city, and it's split into the Northwest, Northeast, Southeast, and Southwest**. You pretty much want to stay in northwest, but that is easy because it is the biggest section. Obviously, you have to go see the monuments, go walk in Georgetown, and of course, you have to take a train up to Baltimore's South Harbor and see a baseball game."

Q "DC is wonderful. Anything you want, it's there. **There are two other universities close by so you'll meet people from there**, too. American University is located in Northwest DC in a very rich/diplomatic suburb area of DC. Everything in DC is within two miles of you at any point. Visit everything! Stay away from Southeast DC!"

Q "American's neighborhood is pretty rich. **There are tons of stores and restaurants**, but some locals might act a little snooty to the college kids. For the most part, though, it's a really nice area."

Q "American is about five miles from Georgetown, but they're mostly snobs there. **We're about 10 miles from the National Mall and downtown DC**. There are endless things to do there. Stay away from Southeast DC, the totally opposite side of the city. It's the ghetto."

Q "You have to go to Georgetown. It's a shopping/eating area on the river with brick streets; it's great. Also visit the National Mall, the museums, and the monuments—especially around Christmas. It's so nice! There are a lot of universities in DC, so **it's a pretty young city, which makes it fun for people our age**."

Q "**Washington is uptight**, a tad on the conservative side behavior-wise, political, and ethnically diverse, (though, largely segregated like many big cities). The city itself is small, but has a lot to offer. Make the Smithsonians and the monuments a priority. Also, see some free performances at the Kennedy Center. Go to the festivals (Taste of DC especially), go shopping in Georgetown, and experience Eastern Market and Adams Morgan. Go to the National Zoo (it's not just for kids!), and go for walks all over the city. People needlessly fear the Shaw neighborhood (home of many jazz clubs, for those of you with cash) and Anacostia (which has the best view of the city, bar none); there's lots of fun to be had in both neighborhoods."

Q "The atmosphere on campus and the neighborhood surrounding **it is calm and suburban**, but there is a charged business in the air that hints that downtown is not far off. The closest universities to AU are the University of the District of Columbia and Georgetown University, but their presence around the campus neighborhood is nonexistent."

Q "DC is what you make of it. If you sit in your dorm and do nothing, then you might as well be living in a cornfield. If you want to drink, go to the frat houses. If you want to go to concerts, there are concerts every day of the week. **I don't believe anyone when they tell me they are bored in DC**."

The College Prowler Take On...
Local Atmosphere

American University is in the northwest quadrant of DC, which, though pretty, doesn't necessarily reflect the fast-paced and urban environment of the city. Fear not—there's truly something for everyone. From the downtown area that is home to every government building imaginable, to the colorful Adams Morgan and Dupont Circle, to the neighborhoods in Southeast that some choose to mistakenly avoid, the city offers clubs, culture, and politics to all those seeking excitement and willing to explore.

DC is considered one of the best college towns in the country, and there is no shortage of young people out to have a great time (or climb the social ladder in hopes of political success). At the same time, AU offers a haven from the intensity in its quiet suburban-type setting, with easy access to I-95 and quainter towns in Maryland and Virginia.

A-

The College Prowler® Grade on
Local Atmosphere: A-

A high Local Atmosphere grade indicates that the area surrounding campus is safe and scenic. Other factors include nearby attractions, proximity to other schools, and the town's attitude toward students.

Safety & Security

The Lowdown On...
Safety & Security

AU Police Phone:
(202) 885-3636 (emergency)
(202) 885-2525 (non-emergency)

Safety Services:
Access control
Americard
Blue-light phones

Health Services:
Located in first floor of McCable Hall

(202) 885-3380
www.american.edu/ocl/healthcenter

Health Center Office Hours:
Monday–Thursday
8 a.m.–6 p.m.,
Friday 8 a.m.–5 p.m.

Did You Know?

AU offers its own **health insurance** to students.

Sibley Hospital is always available to students in an emergency. They are staffed 24 hours a day, 7 days a week, and the ER can be reached at (202) 537-4080.

Students Speak Out On...
Safety & Security

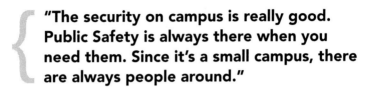

"The security on campus is really good. Public Safety is always there when you need them. Since it's a small campus, there are always people around."

Q "I always felt perfectly safe, even by myself at night. The campus is fairly small and compact, so getting from one side to the other only takes a few minutes. **It's well lit, and the surrounding neighborhood is very nice.** It is right near a lot of embassies, so there's a lot of security off campus as well. The area is patrolled by campus security, DC Metro police, and embassy security. I left my dorm room door unlocked all the time for the two years I lived in the dorms and never had a problem."

Q "**I can tell you that AU's Public Safety department is highly trained** (through the police academy) and capable. On the other hand, they are also mainly in their mid-20s to mid-30s, and they know that you just can't prevent all crime. They take serious infractions seriously—hate crimes, sexual assaults, and the like are infrequent and are sent straight to district authorities for criminal prosecution. The officers have a unique link to the district authorities and often work with Metro PD, Secret Service, and federal agencies when necessary."

Q "Truthfully, it's very safe. It's always lit at night, and really, never empty. **I've walked back to the dorms many times at like 4 a.m., and I'm not scared at all**. I have never had a problem with the safety, and I haven't met someone who has. The only complaint that I have ever heard is that because there really haven't been problems on campus, the security guards are too serious."

Q "Our campus is pretty small, and we do have Public Safety. However, I have heard of incidents that have occurred right outside campus. **You should just be smart enough to not walk alone at night**."

Q "The campus is located on the outskirts of the city. It is the nicest area—very upperclass. **There are really no safety issues at all on campus**; everyone usually gets along well."

Q "The campus is very safe since it's in a more affluent, suburban neighborhood of DC. **It has the feel of a suburban campus with the proximity to all the nightlife of DC**."

Q "**Security is fine, as far, as I can tell**. I mean, I've never been harassed and I don't know any women who have, either. It's not a large campus, so it's kind of easy for Public Safety to patrol it effectively."

Q "AU is a pretty safe place because it is so small and enclosed. **We have campus cops and blue lights for emergencies**. Don't walk alone after like 2 a.m., but I'd say that anywhere."

Q "Security was never really an issue for me, but **the University cops seem to be on top of things**, and they come fast if you call them. We're not in the middle of the city—the school is actually in a really posh suburban area—so crime is not a problem."

Q "**Safety is probably one of AU's finer points**. We're in Northwest DC, only a few minutes from the Vice President's house as well as from many embassies. Many senators and congressmen live in the area. The community is very wealthy, and the campus is very safe; it's not in downtown DC, so if you are looking for a city-block type campus, this isn't it. We have an actual campus, and safety at AU is hardly ever an issue."

Q "The security on campus is really good, and I feel safe walking around at night. **I have never felt scared on campus at all**. Also, the area of DC that American is in is really safe."

Q "They are competent, present, and fortunately for us, **usually unnecessary**."

The College Prowler Take On...
Safety & Security

Being in a more affluent neighborhood means a lower risk for crime at AU. The campus police are visible and effective, providing students with a strong sense of comfort and security. There are blue-light phones available throughout campus in case of emergencies, and security responds quickly and effectively to crises.

In fact, many students think the campus police may be stricter and more vigilant at AU than at other schools because of a lack of serious incidents for them to attend to. In addition, being literally around the block from the Department of Homeland Security and the Japanese and Swedish embassies means the cops are not only looking out for students, but Uncle Sam is as well.

The College Prowler® Grade on
Safety & Security: A

A high grade in Safety & Security means that students generally feel safe, campus police are visible, blue-light phones and escort services are readily available, and safety precautions are not overly necessary.

Computers

The Lowdown On...
Computers

High-Speed Network?
Yes

Wireless Network?
Yes

Number of Labs:
19

Number of Computers:
600

Free Software:
Norton Antivirus

24-Hour Labs:
Yes, the Anderson Computer Lab Sunday–Friday; it closes at midnight on Saturday and reopens Sunday at 8 a.m.

Charge to Print?
Students receive complimentary $25 printing cards; after that, they must cough it up themselves.

Did You Know?

A campus-wide **map of all AU's computing facilities** is available at *www.library.american.edu/about/labs.html.*

Lecture halls have **outlets for laptops** if you want to type your notes.

Students Speak Out On...
Computers

"The computer labs do get kind of crowded, but it depends which building you go to. I would suggest bringing your own computer and printer, but if you can't, there are computers you can use."

Q "The network is usually awesome. **The dorms are wired, and so are the library and cyber café**. One lab is 24-hour, and it's underneath one of the main dorm complexes. There are several other main labs with different, but usually extensive, hours. Just about each school has a lab or two to its name for special software needs. The design program has a design lab; the journalism lab holds PageMaker and Quark. Having your own computer is endlessly convenient, but you don't need to buy one if you haven't done so already."

Q "AU is great about their computer systems. I heard that they're trying to make it a completely wireless campus, including giving everyone cell phones rather than dorm phones. Right now, we have a wireless connection in 48 locations. Also, **all of the dorms are Ethernet wired, and there are computer labs**. I have my own computer (most people here do), so I don't use the computer labs much. But, I am always able to get in at the computer labs whenever I need special software. I recommend having your own computer just because it simplifies everything, but if you don't have one, it won't be a problem."

Q "It's always recommended to bring your own computer, but it's not mandatory. AU also is wireless, which is awesome. You can be anywhere on campus and still be connected to the Internet. If you have your own computer, **some companies give discounts to AU students**."

Q "**There are actually tons of computer labs on campus, so you certainly have your choice**. Yes, the labs do get crowded around midterms and finals, but you can always find one if you need to. The Anderson computer lab, one of the biggest ones, offers free printing of any document, no matter the length, as long as you are an AU student. Nevertheless, I would recommend you bring your own computer. It just makes everything easier and more comfortable for you. You can save all your work on your computer and not on disks or the campus computers. In each dorm, you get free T1 Internet connections, which are fast as hell. That is one of the things I miss, because I moved off campus. The T1 connection is completely free, and you and your roommate each get your own outlet."

Q "**You don't need to bring your own computer**, but it's definitely nice to just have one. Once you get to college, you'll probably talk on Instant Messenger for like 20 hours a day. I'm connected to AIM and the Internet all day long. My computer never shuts off except when I have to do work and need to leave the room. That's another thing; it is better if you have a laptop because you can't always be guaranteed a quiet roommate, and working in the room can be tough."

Q "I never really use the labs. When I did, I had no trouble finding a computer. This is probably because about **80 percent of students have their own computer**, and they only use the lab for special projects. If you can, you should bring your own—it's more convenient, but you don't have to."

Q "The computer network is good. **We have 24-hour hookups in the room** that are separate from the phone lines. There are tons of computer labs and at least one that is open 24-hours. It is nice to have your own computer, but it's not necessary."

Q "The computer labs are acceptable. **The University puts all of its communications online**, so it'd be more convenient to have your own computer, but it's not necessary by any means."

Q "**If you can afford one, bring one (a laptop, to save space)**. If not, it shouldn't be much trouble to find a computer. The Ethernet connection is a blessing and the Internet service failed only two or three times throughout the school year. AU's student Web site *my.american.edu* is a personalized, comprehensive page, which details student accounts and campus activities."

Q "**I'd say 98 percent of people bring their own computer**, many opting for laptops with AU's wireless Internet connection. You can get online almost anywhere on campus without being 'wired up.' Pretty neat. Labs are fine. They're never crowded."

The College Prowler Take On...
Computers

The super-fast Ethernet connection at AU has students wondering why they ever tolerated the trials of dial-up connections. The wireless network is a great convenience for students with laptops who want to emerge from their dorm rooms when writing term papers. This makes buying a laptop the best choice for those bringing their own computers.

Bringing your own computer would be best, but students who can't bring one need not worry; there are plenty of computer labs on campus with Internet access, but some tend to get crowded, so it pays to acquaint yourself with the ones that don't fill up quickly.

B+

The College Prowler® Grade on
Computers: B+

A high grade in Computers designates that computer labs are available, the computer network is easily accessible, and the campus' computing technology is up-to-date.

Facilities

The Lowdown On...
Facilities

Student Center:
Mary Graydon Center

Athletic Center:
Bender Arena

Libraries:
American University Library
AU Media Services
AU Music Library
AU Washington College of
Law Library
Wesley Theological
Seminary Library

Campus Size:
84 acres

Popular Places to Chill:
Mary Graydon Center
Megabytes
The Quad

What Is There to Do on Campus?

Students can go see plays in the Greenberg Theatre, see shows and concerts in the Tavern, watch sports events in Bender Arena, or visit art exhibits in the Watkins Gallery.

Movie Theater on Campus?

No

Bar on Campus?

Yes, in the Tavern

Bowling on Campus?

No

Coffeehouse on Campus?

Yes, Megabytes Café, located underneath the tunnel

Favorite Things to Do

During the spring and early fall, there are often festivals and barbecues on the Quad. During the whole school year, students enjoy getting coffee and ice cream in Megabytes, working out in the fitness center, or going to games and concerts in either the Bender Arena or the Tavern.

Students Speak Out On...
Facilities

"The facilities are fine. I'm not blown away by any of them, but they all certainly meet my needs. AU doesn't have tons of money, so they don't have flashy facilities, but like I said, they always get the job done for me."

Q "**The fitness center is state-of-the-art**, and the track and fields are well-kept."

Q "I would have to say the facilities on campus are really good. **They redid a lot of the buildings**, so there are a lot of new things around campus, such as the Katzen Arts Center, improvements on gym facilities including the William I. Jacobs Recreation Center and Bender Arena, as well as a new SIS building (School of International Services), and the Kogad School of Business renovations."

Q "The gym is free, and the hours are pretty flexible. Also, some of **the sports facilities are open to the students 24/7**. The student center is cool—it has all the little eateries such as the Terrace Dining Room, as well as offices for Greek life, the student-run media group, and other clubs."

Q "**The facilities are really nice**. The classrooms are great; a lot recently got redone. The student center is nice—it's small, but it's good. There are Internet hookups everywhere. The gym is great. It's all pretty new and really nice!"

Q "Facilities on campus are great and are always being improved. Honestly, **the dorms at AU are the nicest that I saw when visiting schools**."

Q "**The facilities are amazing**. They treat us well."

Q "Facilities are very good and **we have a lot of new buildings**. The fitness center is great, but it gets crowded real fast during rush hours, like between 5 p.m.–7 p.m."

Q "The fitness center, cafeteria, and the student center are very nice and have all been recently modernized. The library, several classroom buildings, and some of the dorms are antiquated, but **the campus architecture and facilities all blend the old classical-style** characteristic of Washington with a modern academic look."

Q "The student center is a **collection of food vendors, including Einstein Brothers Bagels**. There are no games (there is a television and lots of seating), but there's a big city out there. There's really no point in having an enormous student center, so we don't have one."

The College Prowler Take On...
Facilities

AU has taken great pains in the past to update and modernize their facilities, but students remain underwhelmed due to the facilities' small sizes. However, most agree that they are good enough, with Internet access and a decent choice in food. Students generally approve of the dorms, and the fitness center is a popular spot and usually crowded with the health-conscious population.

Facilities at AU may not be thrilling, but they are always clean and up-to-date. The city outside is far more attractive to students, which may be why campus life at American is less animated than at other universities.

B

The College Prowler® Grade on
Facilities: B

A high Facilities grade indicates that the campus is aesthetically pleasing and well-maintained; facilities are state-of-the-art, and libraries are exceptional. Other determining factors include the quality of both athletic and student centers and an abundance of things to do on campus.

Campus Dining

The Lowdown On...
Campus Dining

Freshman Meal Plan Requirement?

Yes, students need to get a meal plan consisting of at least 150 blocks, with the regular meal plan being 200 blocks and the super plan being unlimited meals.

Meal Plan Average Cost:

$1,180–$2,025 per semester

Places to Grab a Bite with Your Meal Plan:

Block Express
Food: Boxed lunches to go
Location: Mary Graydon Center
Hours: Monday–Friday
9 a.m.–3 p.m.

Chick-fil-A
Food: Chicken, fast food
Location: Mary Graydon Center
Hours: Monday–Thursday
11 a.m.–11 p.m.,
Friday 11 a.m.–7 p.m.

➜

Eagle's Nest
Food: Conveniece store food
Location: Butler Pavilion
Hours: Monday–Thursday
open 24 hours,
Friday 7 a.m.–10 p.m.,
Saturday 10 a.m.–10 p.m.,
Sunday 10 a.m.–Thursday night

Einstein Bros. Bagels
Food: Bagels, muffins, coffee
Location: Mary Graydon
Center
Hours: Monday–Thursday
7:30 a.m.–5:30 p.m.,
Friday 7:30 a.m.–3 p.m.

Field of Green
Food: Tossed-to-order salads
Location: Mary Graydon
Center
Hours: Monday–Friday
11 a.m.–3 p.m.

Jamba Juice
Food: Smoothies
Location: Sports Center tunnel
adjacent to UPS store
Hours: Monday–Thursday
11 a.m.–11 p.m.,
Friday 11 a.m.–7 p.m.,
Sunday 4 p.m.–11 p.m.

McDonald's
Food: Fast food
Location: Butler Pavilion
Hours: Monday–Saturday
6 a.m.–11 p.m.,
Sunday 7 a.m.–11 p.m.

Megabytes Café
Food: Subs, salads,
sandwiches, ice cream, coffee
Location: Under the tunnel
Hours: Monday–Friday
7 a.m.–11 p.m.,
Saturday–Sunday
10 a.m.–8 p.m.

Pura Vida
Food: Espresso, latte
Location: Mary Graydon
Center
Hours: Monday–Friday
7:30 a.m.–11 p.m.

Salsa
Food: Tex-Mex
Location: Mary Graydon
Center
Hours: Monday–Friday
11 a.m.–3 p.m.

Subway
Food: Sub sandwiches
and salads
Location: Under the tunnel
Hours: Sunday–Thursday
10 a.m.–2 a.m., Friday–
Saturday 10 a.m.–10 p.m.

Tavern
Food: Pizza, burgers, and beer
Location: Mary Graydon
Center, first floor
Hours: Monday–Thursday
11 a.m.–11 p.m.,
Friday 11 a.m.–7 p.m.,
Sunday 4 p.m.–11 p.m.

Terrace Dining Room (TDR)

Food: Comfort food, salads, deli, vegetarian, ice cream, international cuisines

Location: Mary Graydon Center, bottom floor

Hours: Monday–Friday
8 a.m.–3 p.m.,
4:30 p.m.–8 p.m.,
Saturday–Sunday
11 a.m.–3 p.m.,
5 p.m.–7:30 p.m.

Wagshal's American Café

Food: American

Location: Ward Circle Building

Hours: Monday–Thursday
7:30 a.m.–10 p.m.,
Friday 7:30 a.m.–6 p.m.,
Saturday 8 a.m.–4 p.m.

24-Hour On-Campus Eating?

No

Off-Campus Places to Use Your Meal Plan:

Angelico's Pizzeria & Cafe
Armand's Pizzeria
Bagel City Café
Balducci's
Blimpie/TCBY
Blue Diamond Chinese Restaurant
Café Haagen Daaz
Chef Geoff
Domino's Pizza
The Little Cafe/Bistro Med
Manny & Olga's
MotoPhoto
Papa John's Pizza
Philadelphia Cheesesteak Factory
Smoothie Talk
Spring Garden Restaurant
Subway
Taco Bell
Taiwan Café
Tenley Nails
Villa Toscano
Wagshal's Bakery and Catering
Wagshal's Deli
Wagshal's Market
Zebra Lounge/Foster Brothers Coffee

Did You Know?

The comment board in TDR offers **some of the best-hidden comedy**. Make sure to check out students' complaints, and staffers' responses, before you go back to your dorm.

{
"On campus, there's a tavern, a deli, and a minor buffet-style dining hall—all housed in the same building as the Main Hall. There is a McDonald's, a convenience store, and several coffee shops where you can eat."

Q "**Dining Services are now contracted through Bon Appetit**. There's one main dining hall that has an outstanding selection. AU has a diverse ethnic population, and therefore offers diverse cuisine and vegetarian food, as well as the usual things like pizza and burgers."

Q "The food quality went down a little during my four years (or I just got sick of it), but there are a lot of options. **TDR is the main dining hall, and it has a lot of options**, like a salad bar, 'make your own pizza,' and a sandwich bar. You can always find something. There are also smaller specialty places that do sandwiches, soups, and burgers."

Q "**The food is decent**. TDR, which is what we call the main dining hall or Terrace Dining Room, has a pretty good variety of things to eat. Some days are better than others, though, but you can always count on a good salad bar and good fries. There's also the Eagle's Nest, where there is a Subway, and you can also buy some food supplies, too."

Q "There is TDR, Wagshals (which is like a tiny deli in an academic building), the Marketplace (it's on top of TDR, and it is decent), **the Tavern (for fresh burgers, sandwiches, pizza)** and then the Eagle's Nest (a convenience store)."

Q "I personally think that the food is fantastic, especially for a college dining hall. **There is a ton of variety, and they use very fresh ingredients**. Burgers and stir-fry is made to order, and it's all pretty tasty. We have a pay place called the Marketplace, which is where a lot of people hang out during the day. It is all pretty good."

Q "**According to the University, we are ranked sixth in the nation for having the best food**, and I believe it is very accommodating. There is a lot of variety."

Q "Wherever you go, students will tell you that their cafeteria is the worst. Now, I will tell you the same thing, but I will also tell you this: the food here stinks, but it is only because I have been eating here for three years straight. However, I have eaten at other colleges, and their food is far worse than ours. **We have a decent selection of food**, but no matter where you go, you are going to get sick of it."

Q "The food on campus is pretty good. The school has a big cafeteria, which has an all-you-can-eat buffet. It is not the best quality, but it is certainly better than fast food. There are also a couple places on campus that are run by the same company as the cafeteria. The food is a little better, but you can't use your meal plan to buy food like you can in the cafeteria. However, you can use your 'Eagle Bucks' there or pay cash. The way it works is that you sign up for a meal plan in the beginning of the year. Depending on which plan you get, you have a certain amount of meals that you are allowed to eat per semester in the cafeteria. Then you also have Eagle Bucks on your plan. **Eagle Bucks can be used anywhere** on campus and at a lot of places off campus."

Q "TDR, the dining hall, actually isn't bad. They have so many things to choose from, **it's hard not to find something to eat**. There are always vegetarian as well as vegan options offered every single meal. Jamba Juice is another big hit on campus—gotta go there."

Q "Our main cafeteria, **TDR, is rated as one of the best in the country**. It is pretty good, but I always tell people that if you ate at your favorite restaurant every night, you would get sick of it, too. But honestly, it's good; there is always a great salad bar, sandwiches, pizza, pasta, and chicken. Other than TDR, we have a bunch of other good places on campus to get pretty much anything. They all accept Eagle Bucks, which come with your meal plan."

Q "The food isn't terrible, and **the cooks wear cool hats**."

Q "TDR is okay: lots of variety, mediocre execution. **There are food vendors all over campus**, two of which, Jamba Juice and Chick-fil-A, take meal plans."

Q "The food is great and varied, but after eight months, even the best of meals can begin to lose their appeal. There is Subway, McDonald's, and a coffee place, all **good alternatives to cafeteria dining**."

Q "People talk bad about the food at TDR, but **if you stay away from the red meat, it's really not all bad**."

The College Prowler Take On...
Campus Dining

AU's cafeteria is considered much better than typical college fare, featuring unusual multiethnic cuisine and vegetarian and vegan options that are usually very tasty. Students complain more about getting bored with food from the same source throughout their semesters, rather than the quality of the food.

There are other options for those seeking variety—AU has several fast food options, as well as an on-campus convenience store (Eagle's Nest). Students who can afford to fork over a few dollars will do well to venture off campus and try some of DC's many restaurants.

The College Prowler® Grade on

Campus Dining: A-

Our grade on Campus Dining addresses the quality of both school-owned dining halls and independent on-campus restaurants as well as the price, availability, and variety of food.

Off-Campus Dining

The Lowdown On...
Off-Campus Dining

Restaurant Prowler:
Popular Places to Eat!

Afterwords Café
Food: Sandwiches, salads, dessert
1517 Connecticut Ave. NW
(202) 387-1462
www.kramers.com/www/cafemain.htm
Cool Features: Attached to Kramerbooks, a popular independent bookstore in Dupont Circle. Open late!

(Afterwords Café, continued)
Price Range: $3.95–$14.75
Hours: Sunday–Thursday 7:30 a.m.–1 a.m., Friday–Saturday open 24 hours

American City Movie Diner
Food: Typical diner food
5532 Connecticut Ave., NW
(202) 244-1949
www.americancitydiner.com
Cool Features: Retro '50s atmosphere, special dining room where old movies are screened on an 8-by-8 screen.

(American City Movie Diner, continued)

Price: $10–$15

Hours: Sunday–Thursday 7 a.m.–11 p.m., Friday–Saturday open 24 hours.

Armand's Chicago-Style Pizza

Food: Famous deep Dish pizza or traditional style, wings, salad, subs

1140 19th St .NW #200

(202) 331-9500

www.armandspizza.com

Cool Features: Fast delivery.

Price: $5–10 per person

Hours: Open daily from 11 a.m.–12 a.m.

Buca Di Beppo

Food: Italian

1825 Connecticut Ave, NW

(202) 232-8466

Cool Features: Family-sized portions, wacky old photographs and artwork on the walls.

Price: $15–$20 per person

Hours: Sunday 4 p.m.–9 p.m., Monday–Friday 5 p.m.–10 p.m., Saturday 4 p.m.–11 p.m.

Chef Geoff's

Food: Gourmet

3201 New Mexico Ave., NW

(202) 237-7800

www.chefgeoff.com

Cool Features: Live jazz band during Sunday brunch every week.

Price: $25–$35 per person

(Chef Geoff's, continued)

Hours: Monday–Saturday 11:30 a.m.–11 p.m., bar open until 12 a.m., Sunday 10:30 a.m.–3 p.m., 4 p.m.–10 p.m., bar open until 12 a.m.

Chipotle Mexican Grill

Food: Mexican

1837 M St., NW

(202) 466-4104

www.chipolte.com

Cool Features: Very fresh ingredients.

Price: $7–$12 per person

Hours: Open daily from 11 a.m.–10 p.m.

Guapo's

Food: Mexican

4515 Washington Ave., NW

(202) 686-3588

Cool Features: Known for their margaritas and fajitas.

Price: $10–$20 per person

Hours: Sunday–Thursday 11:30 a.m.–11 p.m., Friday–Saturday 11:30 a.m.–12 a.m.

Lebanese Taverna

Food: Lebanese/Middle Eastern

2641 Connecticut Ave., NW

(202) 265-8681

www.lebanesetaverna.com/ restaurants/dc

Cool Features: In fashionable Woodley Park.

Price: $12–$25 per person

(Lebanese Taverna, continued)

Hours: Monday 5:30 p.m.–
10 p.m., Tuesday–Thursday
11:30 a.m.–2:30 p.m.,
5:30 p.m.–10 p.m., Friday–
Saturday 11 a.m.–3 p.m.,
5:30 p.m.–11 p.m.

The Old Ebbitt Grill

Food: American

675 15 St., NW

(202) 347-4800

www.ebbitt.com

Cool Features: Best burgers
in town.

Price: $15–$30 per person

Hours: Monday–Friday
7:30 a.m.–1 a.m., bar open
until 2 a.m.,
Saturday–Sunday 8:30 a.m.–
1 a.m., bar open until 3 a.m.

Tastee Diner

Food: American

118 Washington Blvd.,
Bethesda MD

(301) 953-7567

www.tasteediner.com

Cool Features: Breakfast
served 24 hours a day.

Price: $8–$12 per person

Hours: Open 24 hours a day

Tono Sushi

Food: Japanese

2605 Connecticut Ave., NW

(202) 332-7300

www.tonosushi.com

Cool Features: "Americanized"
menu options. Lunch specials
daily.

Price: $12–$25 per person

Hours: Monday–Thursday
11:30 a.m.–2:30 p.m.,
5 p.m.–10 p.m.,
Friday 11:30 a.m.–
2:30 p.m., 5 p.m.–11 p.m.,
Saturday 12 p.m.–3 p.m.,
5 p.m.–11 p.m.,
Sunday 12 p.m.–3 p.m.,
5 p.m.–10 p.m.

Other Places to Check Out:

Angelico's

Billy Martin's Tavern

Cafe Deluxe

Daily Grille

The Diner

J Paul's

Krupin's

McCormick & Schmidt's

McDonald's

Ruby Tuesday's

Starbuck's

Steak and Eggs

Third Edition

Best Burgers:
The Old Ebbitt Grill

Best Sushi:
Tono Sushi

Best Breakfast:
Tastee Diner

Best Healthy:
Afterwords Café

Best Place to Take Your Parents:
Buca di Beppo

Student Favorites:
Guapo's

The Old Ebbit Grill

Tastee Diner

Plus, the Adams Morgan neighborhood is home to many immigrants, and therefore a wide array of foreign fare, especially Middle Eastern and Ethiopian food.

Closest Grocery Stores:
Fresh Fields
4530 40th St. NW
(202) 237-5800

Safeway Food & Drug: Washington Stores
1855 Wisconsin Ave. NW
(202) 333-3223

Giant
5400 Westbard Ave., Bethesda
(301) 652-1484

Whole Foods Market
1440 P St. NW
(202) 332-4300

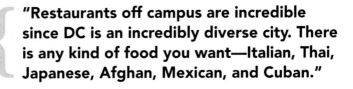

Students Speak Out On...
Off-Campus Dining

> "Restaurants off campus are incredible since DC is an incredibly diverse city. There is any kind of food you want—Italian, Thai, Japanese, Afghan, Mexican, and Cuban."

Q "**Restaurants in DC are out of this world**, although somewhat unfulfilling to certain palates—one of my roommates is a native Californian and only found restaurants he liked in our second semester."

Q "There are a bunch of great restaurants in Georgetown and downtown DC. **The only thing is they are generally on the expensive side**, so being a poor college student like myself, it's rare to really go out and eat."

Q "Right around campus **we have Chipotle (Mexican), Armand's (Pizza), Chef Geoff's (Bistro)**, Starbucks, Guapo's (Mexican), and Krupin's (Deli) just to name a few."

Q "They just put a Ruby Tuesday's close to campus, and there is another place called Steak and Eggs. It is a grease bucket and it only sits around 10 people, but it is the best food. Plus, it is open 24 hours, so it really is the favorite spot for kids around here. **All these places are pretty cheap, so if you have $20 in your pocket, you're set**."

Q "Right near campus there are a lot of good options; if you **take the Metro**, you can easily get to all of the amazing restaurants."

Q "I really like Chef Geoff's—an 'American Cuisine' place that has many AU students on staff. If you're experienced, it's a great place to work and very lucrative. There's also Cafe Deluxe, which is a fifteen-minute walk from campus. Armand's makes a great Chicago-style pizza, and the Dupont Circle area is full of awesome places. **Truthfully, it's hard to find a really bad restaurant here**."

Q "DC is a great city with lots of places to eat. There is a place called Dupont Circle that has an amazing variety of dining options. From Thai, to Greek, to Indian, to Mexican, to French, to Italian—it's all here. **Some places are more expensive than others, but I love spending money on good times**."

Q "Of course, there are some great places near school in Friendship Heights, and **right near campus the best places are Chef Geoff's, Guapo's, Mickey D's, a Thai place, and Armand's**. And of course, there's my personal favorite, Chipotle. If you like Mexican food—simple burritos and tacos—you'll love Chipotle."

Q "**The restaurants are superior**, especially J. Paul's in Georgetown, the Old Ebbit Grill by the White House, McCormick & Schmick's, the Daily Grille in Georgetown and Dupont, Third Edition and Billy Martin's Tavern in Georgetown. But the best place for cheap eats is the Tastee Diner in Bethesda, MD."

Q "**There's too many places to name**. If you like diners, there's a trendy one with a not-at-all-clever name in Adams Morgan (The Diner), and a grungy one with a cult following in Bethesda, Maryland (Tastee Diner). Mexican food in Tenleytown at Guapos: not bad. Good pizza at Angelico's."

The College Prowler Take On...
Off-Campus Dining

It seems that every country in the world has not only an embassy in DC, but also a restaurant. The more adventurous your tastes run, the more fun you'll have exploring the city's cuisine. Be careful though, pricey menus have been known to hurt students' already notoriously thin wallets.

However, there are cheap eats if you know where to look. Tenleytown and nearby Bethesda, MD have all-night diners that are popular hangouts for college students, and there are plenty of places with free delivery. AU students stress that going deeper into the city is key to sample the international culture.

The College Prowler® Grade on
Off-Campus Dining: A

A high Off-Campus Dining grade implies that off-campus restaurants are affordable, accessible, and worth visiting. Other factors include the variety of cuisine and the availability of alternative options (vegetarian, vegan, Kosher, etc.).

Campus Housing

The Lowdown On...
Campus Housing

Room Types:
Doubles, suites, and
(a few) singles

Best Dorms:
Centennial

Hughes

Worst Dorms:
Anderson

**Undergrads Living
on Campus:**
75%

**Number of
Dormitories:**
9

**Number of University-
Owned Apartments:**
1

→

Dormitories:

North Complexes:

Hughes
Floors: 7

Total Occupancy: 260

Bathrooms: Single-sex communal

Coed: Five coed floors, and two all-female floors

Residents: Freshmen and upperclassmen

Room Types: Doubles, triples

Special Features: Known for its strong sense of community, bottom floor is a computer cluster; houses two Honors floors; each room individually controls their air conditioning and heat; TV lounges; laundry facilities.

Leonard
Floors: 8

Total Occupancy: 280

Bathrooms: Single-sex communal

Coed: Five coed, two all-female floors

Residents: Freshmen and upperclassmen

Room Types: Doubles

Special Features: International/intercultural hall, in which multiculturalism is a primary focus; bottom floor is a computer cluster; each room individually controls their air-conditioning and heat; TV lounges; laundry facilites.

McDowell
Floors: 7

Total Occupancy: 250

Bathrooms: Single-sex communal

Coed: Five coed floors, two all-female floors

Residents: Freshmen and upperclassmen

Room Types: Singles, suites, doubles, triples

Special Features: Houses the North Side Fitness Center; computer cluster on bottom floor; each room individually controls their air-conditioning and heat; TV lounges; laundry facilities; includes community service and wellness floors.

South Complexes:

Anderson
Floors: 7

Total Occupancy: 300

Bathrooms: Single-sex communal

Coed: Yes, all floors

Residents: Freshmen and upperclassmen

Room Types: Doubles

Special Features: Houses more students than any other hall; has an Honors hall; several Greek Chapter rooms; South Side Computer lab is on bottom floor.

Centennial

Floors: 6

Total Occupancy: 260

Bathrooms: Semi-private

Coed: Yes, all floors

Residents: Upperclassmen

Room Types: Suites

Special Features: Only dorm reserved strictly for upperclassmen.

Letts

Floors: 6

Total Occupancy: 250

Bathrooms: Single-sex communal

Coed: Five coed floors, one all-female floor

Residents: Freshmen and upperclassmen

Room Types: Doubles

Special Features: Second-largest hall; houses the Community Service floor and an Honors floor; South Campus Fitness Center is located in hall, as is the Game and Recreation Center.

Tenley Campus:

Congressional Hall

Floors: 3

Total Occupancy: 160

Bathrooms: Single-sex communal

Coed: Yes

Residents: Freshmen and upperclassmen

Room Types: Doubles

(Congressional Hall, continued)

Special Features: Staffed 24 hours a day, is where all the residents of Tenley Campus check in, and where students catch the shuttle to the main campus.

Capital Hill

Floors: 5

Total Occupancy: 194

Bathrooms: Single-sex communal

Coed: Yes

Residents: Freshmen and upperclassmen

Room Types: Doubles

Special Features: Oldest and most ornate hall boasting wide marble staircase and high ceilinged rooms; houses the Tenley Fitness Center.

Federal Hall

Floors: 3

Total Occupancy: 105

Bathrooms: Single-sex communal

Coed: Yes

Residents: Freshmen and upperclassmen

Room Types: Doubles

Special Features: Contains the mail room; cafeteria on the first floor.

Park Bethesda

Floors: 9

Total Occupancy: 516

Bathrooms: Private

Coed: Yes, in building, not in apartments

Residents: Juniors, seniors, and transfer students

Room Types: Studio, one bedroom, two bedroom, and loft units

Special Features: Located close to two grocery stores, a drug store, Starbuck's, two banks, dry cleaners, restaurants, and other stores; parking leases are available at a cost.

Bed Type
Twin

Cleaning Service?
Bathrooms, lounges, and hallways are cleaned by a professional staff, while cleaning the individual dorm rooms is up to the students.

Students Speak Out On...
Campus Housing

{ "The dorms are so nice. They have carpeting, wall units, air-conditioning, and the two largest dorms are connected. Living in Anderson or Letts is probably the best option if you like to party and have the real college experience."

Q "Dorms on the south side are Anderson, Letts, and Centennial. They are known to be big, loud, and fun. Dorms on the north side of campus are McDowell, Hughes, and an international dorm. They are smaller and quieter but still fun. In general, **dorms aren't that small, and many have cool wall units**, two beds, and two desks."

Q "The dorms were better than most college dorms I've seen. I lived in Anderson, on the south side of campus. I am biased and think that the south side dorms— **Anderson, Letts, Centennial—are better to live in, in terms of the people and atmosphere**. All of the dorms are decent, though."

Q "**If you want an international community, go with Leonard Hall**. McDowell and Hughes are quiet and tend to attract the Honors students. These are all on the north side. On the south side, you have the Letts/Anderson complex, which includes the Centennial upperclassmen suites. Letts is a dump, Anderson is fun and friendly, and Centennial is for serious students or those with internships and little time for hanging out. I wouldn't recommend it until you build up a base of friends and can move there with people you know."

Q "The dorms are pretty decent. **They have communal bathrooms and kitchens**, which you do eventually get used to. If you want a close-knit community, I would suggest living on the north side just because the buildings are smaller. If you want a crazy party scene, you should live on the south side."

Q "The dorms are very nice. There are north and south sides of campus, both with a different atmosphere. **The north side is quieter—no Greeks, but more athletes and international students**. These dorms are Hughes, Leonard, and McDowell. The south side is more outgoing and fun with people always outside hanging out. There are more Greeks and more parties. These dorms are Letts, Anderson, and Centennial, which is for upperclassmen only."

Q "**The dorms are nice, but RAs suck**. If you like to hang out and party, go for Centennial, Letts, or Anderson. Your fourth choice should be McDowell, but just avoid Leonard."

Q "The dorms are fine. **Anderson and Letts are considered to be the social dorms**. Hughes and McDowell are quieter, and Leonard houses a lot of the international students and has been known to get loud."

Q "**All the rooms are the same, and they're all pretty nice, though a little on the small side**. We have two sides, north and south. The south side is a lot crazier and a lot more fun, but it is also a little dirtier. I would still recommend living in Anderson, though; you'll have a blast. Avoid Letts; it's kind of dingy, but it's still fun. On the north side is Hughes (avoid this one at all costs; it's very boring), McDowell (it's nice, but quiet and has lots of athletes), and Leonard (it's the international dorm and actually a lot of fun, with really interesting people). Live in Leonard if you want to have a different experience."

Q "**Dorms suck**, dude . . . seriously. They suck."

Q "Dorms are dorms, pretty basic, with lots of storage space. **Like parties? Move to Anderson or Letts. Don't? Move to Hughes**."

Q "For the **best combination of zany coed dorm life and quiet collegiate life**, pick a dorm on the north side of campus, like Hughes, McDowell, or Leonard. Centennial has suites and higher-class rooms, but is usually only available to upperclassmen. Letts and Anderson form a giant, connected dorm megaplex, which I affectionately call the 'Jungle.' Don't go without a broadsword."

Q "**Dorms are relatively nice and are cleaned by a service almost everyday**. It's nice that we have a kitchen on every floor, and it's cleaned for us. Just remember that north side (Leonard, Hughes, and McDowell) are considered the quieter dorms, but are by no means boring. Leonard is the international hall, but you don't have to be an international student to live there. Many of my friends have great experiences there. South side tends to be a bit rowdier, with many of the sororitiy sisters and frat brothers occupying the rooms. But be warned—the fire alarms will go off . . . and during rush . . . all the time . . . 2 p.m., 2 a.m. . . . all the time."

The College Prowler Take On...
Campus Housing

AU dorms cater to students of varied dispositions. The north side dorms of Hughes, McDowell, and Leonard are considered quieter, but residents there say they have tight-knit communities because they are smaller. The south side dorms, Letts, Anderson, and Centennial, are home to more frat brothers and sorority sisters, and are therefore a little rowdier.

Leonard is an international dorm, and there are specialized floors elsewhere, including all-women floors and community service floors. Most students are satisfied with housing options, as long as they live somewhere appropriate to their personalities. Many freshmen live on campus and say it makes meeting people easier, but by junior year, some students start moving off campus.

B

The College Prowler® Grade on
Campus Housing: B

A high Campus Housing grade indicates that dorms are clean, well-maintained, and spacious. Other determining factors include variety of dorms, proximity to classes, and social atmosphere.

Off-Campus Housing

The Lowdown On...
Off-Campus Housing

Undergrads in Off-Campus Housing:
25%

Average Rent For:
Studio Apt.: $800/per month
1BR Apt.: $1,000/per month
2BR Apt.: $1,700/per month

Popular Areas:
Bethesda
Friendship Heights
Tenleytown

For Assistance Contact:
www.american.edu/ocl/ housing
(202) 885-3370
housinganddiningweb@ american.edu

Best Time to Look For a Place:
A couple of months before you want to move in.

Students Speak Out On...
Off-Campus Housing

"You have to pretty much look for off-campus housing by yourself, but I don't think it's very hard because there are a lot of apartments around the area."

Q "**The buildings are old, so you'll want to be careful when looking around**. Also, AU recently purchased apartments in several local buildings which are used as on-campus housing, so you might want to look into that. Trust me, if you're working on financial aid and money you've saved up, it can be easier to go through the school than to pay rent each month. When you look up apartment rents, though, remember that utilities are often included in the rent, which is different from the places I lived in before."

Q "There are a lot of available apartments, but **living in a city is pricey**."

Q "**Housing is expensive off and on campus**. I'm dealing with that now. Next year, I'll be living in AU's Park Bethesda Apartments (their upperclassman and graduate student apartments) just outside the DC border in Maryland. That will probably cost me almost $1,000 a month, though. If you look hard, you should be able to find something for about $700 a month."

Q "Off-campus housing is decent. I lived off campus for two years and really enjoyed it. It's expensive (like everything in DC), but **there are a fair number of apartments and rental houses near campus**. The Metro makes AU pretty accessible, so even if you live farther from campus, it's still easy to get there."

Q "**Housing off campus can actually be cheaper than on-campus housing**. At school, it's $750 to share a 200-square-foot room with someone else. Off campus, for $750 you can get your own bedroom, living room, kitchen, and still have a roommate in the nice apartments down the street."

Q "**I can't recommend living off campus because it is too expensive for college students**. Sometimes people have to squeeze six people into a place in order for it to be reasonably priced."

Q "The housing off campus is very nice because you will be looking in northwest Washington, DC. There are some ritzy places. **There is usually always a way to get to school from any point in DC**, so don't worry about that. You might have to take a bus to a Metro and then the Metro to Tenley, but you'll get there."

Q "There are a lot of apartment buildings and housing around campus. **Living in DC can be very expensive, but you can always find a good deal somewhere**."

Q "**Near campus, there are two huge apartment buildings about a block away**. Be aware that living off campus in DC is very expensive. A one-bedroom apartment can range from $1,000–$1,500. Some friends and I are renting a house near campus starting in June. The rent is $2,400 a month for the three of us. This is pretty much the best off-campus deal. We all have our own bedrooms and a cool house. Plus, the rent is only about $200 more than what it costs to live on campus."

Q "It's expensive, but easily accessible. All freshmen, the majority of sophomores, and about a third of the juniors live on campus. **It's just cheaper and easier that way**."

Q "Housing off campus is pretty easy, but **most people don't move off until junior year**."

Q "Off-campus housing is expensive, **but the University owns some properties that are decent** and worth looking into."

Q "There is little off campus housing at AU; it is limited and they do make it easy to find **convenient and affordable alternative solutions**."

Q "**Live on campus, meet new people** . . . Move off sophomore or junior year. It's a valuable experience."

The College Prowler Take On...
Off-Campus Housing

Finding suitable and affordable off-campus housing in a decent neighborhood can be a huge headache for students, and they often find they must have one or more roommates to swing an apartment or house. Despite this, a significant amount of upperclassmen choose to leave campus. One pro to off-campus life is that in DC, you're never too far from a Metro, so you can find your way to AU for classes quite easily.

In response to sky-high rents in DC, AU offers University-sponsored off-campus living options, in the Park Bethesda and Grover-Tunlaw apartment buildings, that don't cost much more than the dorms. These locations are becoming more popular.

The College Prowler® Grade on
Off-Campus Housing: D+

A high grade in Off-Campus Housing indicates that apartments are of high quality, close to campus, affordable, and easy to secure.

Diversity

The Lowdown On...
Diversity

Native American:
Less than 1%

White:
77%

Asian American:
5%

International:
7%

African American:
6%

Out-of-State:
78%

Hispanic:
5%

Political Activity

College Democrats, College Republicans, College Libertarians, as well as many specialized political activist groups and clubs.

Gay Pride

Two words: very acceptive. The GLBTA Resource center takes an active role in helping AU students find GLBTA related volunteer, internship, and study abroad opportunities.

Economic Status

Mostly middle- to upper-middle-class.

Sample Minority Clubs

Black Student Alliance, Latin American Student Organization, and Muslim Students Association.

Most Popular Religions

The school is affiliated with the United Methodist church.

Students Speak Out On...
Diversity

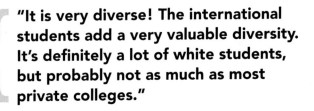

"It is very diverse! The international students add a very valuable diversity. It's definitely a lot of white students, but probably not as much as most private colleges."

Q "It's extremely diverse. We have an enormous international population, which is one of the reasons I came here. Many of them are diplomats' kids, and **we get a few minor royals from time to time**."

Q "It's more diverse than I ever thought it could be. **You honestly will meet people from countries you have never heard of**. My freshman year, I learned how to say things like 'Hello, how are you?' and 'Can I have a cigarette?' in like 14 languages. It's great, especially in the summer when most of the international kids don't go home and stay here to take classes. There are a lot of Arab people, North Africans, Europeans, and Asians, but there are not so many South Americans or Australians."

Q "The campus is very diverse. **There is a large international population**, as well as many Jewish kids. While it is mostly Caucasians, American is known for diversity. It is one of the main reasons I came to this school."

Q "They claim that it's really diverse, but I don't think it is. **The different groups sort of stick together** and there are a lot of rich kids from the New York and New Jersey areas."

Q "AU is diverse nationally and internationally, but **not as much racially or economically**. The AU administration is hell-bent on making the school the most diverse, international American campus in the history of the world, which, I guess, is good. But it might be better to tune up the academic curriculum first."

Q "Compared to other colleges, it's fairly diverse. Compared to the city in which AU is situated, **it's not diverse at all**."

Q "While American can be diverse, **it depends on your definition/interpretation** of the word diversity."

Q "The best way to experience the diversity of AU is to **live in the international dorm (Leonard)**."

The College Prowler Take On...
Diversity

When examining diversity, it depends what one considers diverse. Religiously, AU students come from many different backgrounds. Economically, scholarships offered provide some variety, but most students are from middle- to upper-middle-class homes. Location-wise, they hail from all 50 states and over 100 foreign countries, and AU prides itself on the booming international student population.

However, a majority of students are white, and some say they expected to see more minority students on campus. Considering how culturally and racially diverse DC is, AU is not a great reflection of that. There are many gay students, which creates a comfortable and accepting atmosphere, as well as many from the northeastern United States.

The College Prowler® Grade on

Diversity: C-

A high grade in Diversity indicates that ethnic minorities and international students have a notable presence on campus and that students of different economic backgrounds, religious beliefs, and sexual preferences are well-represented.

Guys & Girls

The Lowdown On...
Guys & Girls

Men Undergrads:
38%

Women Undergrads:
62%

Birth Control Available?

Yes, in the Health Center

Social Scene

The social scene at AU is varied—there's something for everyone. However, AU has an overwhelming female population. Therefore, many of the more attractive young women on campus either lower their standards—looks-wise—or choose to head off-campus to find an equally attractive male counterpart. Ladies, do not fear, though—DC is full of eligible bachelors. Be sure to check out the frat and house parties, clubs, bars, and shows in the area.

Hookups or Relationships?

Hookups are definitely more common. AU students are too busy for relationships.

Best Place to Meet Guys/Girls

Out in the city! Don't stick to AU.

Dress Code

It's casual but stylish. Individuality is key—it's important to stand out if you want to snag a boyfriend or girlfriend!

Did You Know?

Top Three Places to Find Hotties:
1. Clubs like Nation and Platinum
2. Bars and restaurants in popular neighborhoods like Adams Morgan
3. Your own dorm

Top Five Places to Hook Up:
1. The amphitheater
2. Courtyard between Hughes and McDowell
3. The stairwells in dorms
4. Davenport Lounge
5. Your own dorm room

Students Speak Out On...
Guys & Girls

> "The guys on campus don't particularly overwhelm me, but there are so many different kinds of people at AU. If you haven't met people you like, just wait five minutes."

Q "The guys that I know are really chill and a lot of fun. **You get a mix of people, so I'm sure you won't have a hard time finding guy friends**. The girls that I know are really great. I made some really good friends here. I'm really picky about guys, but I'm sure there are some goodies on campus."

Q "The way I look at it is that, on the hotness scale, people tend to go from extreme to extreme. **They're either really hot or really, really not**."

Q "My overall take on the student body is that they are diverse (in terms of interests, culture, where they come from, and goals), smart, politically and socially aware, and nice. Lots of AU people go into the Peace Corps or other service programs after college. Lots work on Capitol Hill or for other government agencies. **I am constantly impressed with the people I meet**."

Q "Oh, dear, didn't anyone tell you? **AU is overwhelmingly female**. Of the small male population, a near majority are gay. However, don't be too discouraged. They're all nice, and the town is crawling with undergrads, Congressional staffers, interns, and law students. There is no shortage of eligible men, and they are indeed hot—East Coast style, though. Be forewarned."

Q "There are definitely good-looking people here. There are also people that think they are too good-looking. But seriously, **it is a nice-looking campus**."

Q "Truth be told, **there is a decent amount of gay guys**. I guess there are some decent-looking guys around, but the ratio of girls to guys at AU is like 60/40. I don't complain, though."

Q "**The dating scene is whack**. But that may just be my unfortunate experience."

Q "Sane straight guys are in short supply, but **there are plenty of potheads**, thugs, alcoholics, and hipster doofuses. The gay population at AU is big, but not as big as I think many people have exaggerated it to be. But the campus is, from my observation, completely accepting. As for the girls, there are possibly twice as many of them as guys, and they are, for the most part, better at being friends than the gentlemen on campus. There is also a high percentage of both guys and girls who are activists, or believe in something that they feel will make people talk about them."

Q "**Soooooooooo many girls** . . . guys, well, they are a bit outnumbered, and often 'not interested,' but there are always two or three in your classes."

Q "You will hear that most guys are Jewish and/or gay . . . which has some truth behind it. In any matter, they are usually rich and from New Jersey, or somewhere on the East Coast. **Girls are usually Jewish New Jersey dwellers**, as well."

The College Prowler Take On...
Guys & Girls

Fear not: you don't have to look like a supermodel to find a mate at AU. The cosmopolitan and ambitious student body tends to place a greater emphasis on individuality, motivation, and intelligence than on appearance, but a fresh, clean-cut look doesn't hurt either.

Straight women at AU complain that satisfactory boyfriends are hard to find, as girls vastly outnumber the guys on campus. Plus, there is a notable gay population. Exploring the greater city may be a more efficient way to hook up. Don't be afraid to go out and meet people at bars, clubs, city organizations, or just on the street.

The College Prowler® Grade on
Guys: B-

A high grade for Guys indicates that the male population on campus is attractive, smart, friendly, and engaging, and that the school has a decent ratio of guys to girls.

The College Prowler® Grade on
Girls: A-

A high grade for Girls not only implies that the women on campus are attractive, smart, friendly, and engaging, but also that there is a fair ratio of girls to guys.

Athletics

The Lowdown On...
Athletics

Athletic Division:
Division I

Conference:
Patriot League

School Mascot:
Clawed the Eagle

School Colors:
Red, white, and blue

**Males Playing
Varsity Sports:**
115 (5%)

**Female Playing
Varsity Sports:**
139 (4%)

➜

Men's Varsity Sports:

Basketball

Cross-Country

Golf

Soccer

Swimming & Diving

Tennis

Track & Field

Wrestling

Women's Varsity Sports:

Basketball

Cross-Country

Field Hockey

Lacrosse

Soccer

Swimming & Diving

Tennis

Track & Field

Volleyball

Club Sports:

Crew

Cycling

Equestrian

Gymnastics

Ice Hockey (Women's)

Rugby (Men's, Women's)

Sailing

Softball

Soccer (Women's)

Ultimate Frisbee (Men's)

Intramurals:

Basketball (Indoor, Outdoor)

Dodgeball

Flag Football

Soccer (Indoor)

Softball

Volleyball (Court, Sand)

Tennis

Ultimate Frisbee

Athletic Fields

Reeves Field/Greenberg Track

Getting Tickets

Just go to the Bender Arena box office, and you will get free tickets by showing your student ID.

Most Popular Sports

Basketball, volleyball, and soccer

Overlooked Teams

Cycling and women's rugby do quite well, yet their success goes largely unnoticed by the student body.

Best Place to Take a Walk

Rock Creek Park, the Nebraska Avenue dog park

Gyms/Facilities

American Outdoor Tennis Courts

American University features seven outdoor tennis courts for the use of the intercollegiate tennis teams as well as the University community. Two outdoor basketball courts complete the outdoor recreational facility located next to Reeves Field and behind Bender Arena. The three-month project gave the University one of the finest outdoor surfaces in the area.

Bender Arena

The 300,000 square foot building connects to the Mary Graydon Center to create an enormous hub of student activity. Commencement, concerts, basketball and volleyball games, guest speakers, and camps and high school basketball games take place here.

Jacobs Fitness Center

In Jacobs, you'll find dumbell weights, weight machines, treadmills, Stairmasters, bikes, a pool, and much more.

Reeves Athletic Complex and Greenberg Track

Utilized as a soccer and lacrosse competition site, Reeves Field has gained notoriety throughout the collegiate and professional ranks as one of the finest fields in the nation. Reeves Field also features a six-lane track to accommodate the track and field programs at AU. The exclusive soccer pitch conforms to both NCAA and international standards with a roomy 74 x 117 yard playing surface.

Reeves Aquatic Center

Includes two pools—one 20-feet, and the other 25-feet in length. Recreation hours can be found by calling (202) 885-6267.

Students Speak Out On...
Athletics

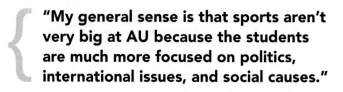

"My general sense is that sports aren't very big at AU because the students are much more focused on politics, international issues, and social causes."

Q "It's not a big rah-rah school spirit place, but it's becoming more so. **Intramural (IM) sports are bigger**—lots of people participate, but it's not expected that you'll do them."

Q "**We don't have a football team**. Enough said, right? We have great soccer and basketball teams, though."

Q "Just this year, **the sports at school got really big**—especially our basketball team. All our sports teams are really good, though, and the games are a lot of fun."

Q "**Sports are pretty much non existent here**. Basketball was big this year because we did well, but that's about it. No one else really watches or cares about our school's athletics program."

Q "There is lacrosse, soccer, swimming, diving, and rugby as varsity-type sports, and then there are club teams for roller-hockey, hockey, and the like. Personally, I think that **fraternity flag football is more exhilarating than any actual University sport**."

Q "**Intramurals at AU are like Greek life** in that, if you want nothing to do with them, nobody will look at you any different. Varsity sports and other activities are only as big as you want them to be. I remember my freshman year, the guys on my floor made a soccer team. I didn't join—nobody looked down on me. It just wasn't my thing. Again, sports and Greek life are only as big as you want them to be."

Q "Both varsity and IM sports are big on campus. **AU is Division I, so we are totally into our basketball team**. However, we don't have a football team at all."

Q "AU sport life is weak. No one really cares. We don't have a football team anymore. Our basketball team almost made it to the NCAA tournament once, but they lost a heartbreaker in the qualifying game to Holy Cross. Other than that, **our volleyball and soccer teams are pretty good**. We have a new athletics coordinator and he's trying to make athletics more important on campus; they have been improving."

Q "Sports aren't as big as they should be, but **they have grown in popularity over the last couple of years**. AU is not an athletically-oriented campus like Notre Dame or Penn State, but the varsity teams are Division I, and for the meager funding and publicity they get, they are quite good, especially women's volleyball, the soccer teams, and the men's basketball team. IM sports are not big, and they are poorly run by the athletics department, but they are mostly fun, nonetheless."

Q "**Sports are largely ignored**, which is surprising for a Division I school."

Q "Our varsity sports do not get the recognition they deserve. Some of our teams (lacrosse, soccer, basketball, just to name a few) do extremely well but are **never mentioned**, which is too bad. IM sports are there, but hopefully will become larger."

The College Prowler Take On...
Athletics

AU isn't exactly known for its school spirit. Though the sports teams are Division I, and there are ample intramural teams, many students are less enthused about going to games than going out into DC. Many of the bigger sports fans on campus complain about the absence of a football team—they claim that this contributes to the lack of school spirit on campus.

Some students are trying to get their peers more excited—a recently founded club, the Screaming Eagles, go all out at the games, painting their faces, and coming up with their own cheers. Basketball and volleyball are popular sports, and in the rare instance where a game is being televised, the turnout is better than usual.

The College Prowler® Grade on

Athletics: C

A high grade in Athletics indicates that students have school spirit, that sports programs are respected, that games are well-attended, and that intramurals are a prominent part of student life.

Nightlife

The Lowdown On...
Nightlife

Club and Bar Prowler: Popular Nightlife Spots!

Club Crawler

Daedalus

1010 Vermont Ave, NW

(202) 347-9066

www.clubdaedalus.com

Daedalus plays hip-hop, dance, and techno; the dress code is upscale; and it features a sunken dance floor.

FUR

33 Patterson St. NE

(202) 842-3401

www.furnightclub.com

Open Thursday–Saturday, FUR has three rooms—the main room or the arena, a martini lounge, a mafia room, and the mink lounge. Thursdays host all types of music, Fridays are ladies nights—ladies are admitted for free (18-or-older for females, 21-or-older for males), and host hip hop,

(FUR, continued)

house, international, and latin rhythms. Saturday hosts a different DJ in all four rooms, and tickets may be sold in advance, sometimes costing $20. Dress sophisticated and chic—there is a dress code.

Love

1350 Okie St., NE

(202) 636-9030

www.lovetheclub.com

Music at Love is international, hip hop, and dance; dress is upscale; and it features several levels, a diverse crowd, and often has theme nights throughout the week. Check out its Web site. The cover varies, and it is 21-and-over.

Nation

1015 Half St., SE

(202) 554-1500

A great venue for bands, Nation has hosted big names such as Limp Bizkit, 311, NOFX, David Bowie, Lenny Kravitz, Rage Against the Machine, and Ozzy Ozzbourne. Its size exceeds any other club in DC, with three indoor levels, and a multi-level outdoor patio area.

Platinum

915 F St., NW

(202) 393-3555

www.platinumclubdc.com

Platinum is the biggest 18-and-

(Platinum, continued)

over college club venue, featuring five levels, two dance floors, and a VIP room with fabric hanging down from the ceiling. Open Thursdays– Sundays, check in to see if there are any guest celebrities, and dance to hip-hop, trance, R&B, house, and check out the DJs. Dress fashionably; there is a dress code.

Polly Esther's

605 12th St., NW

(202) 737-1970

www.pollyesthers.com

Fans of disco music and the 1970s continue to turn out in droves to celebrate the decade. With Saturday Night Fever and Twister dance floors, a full-size replica of the "Partridge Family" bus, a drink menu that includes libations like Brady Punch, Polly Esther's is the first choice of clubgoers looking for a great time. Open only three nights a week— Thursday, Friday and Saturday, with other nights open for private parties and special events.

Bar Prowler:

Asylum

2471 18 St., NW

(202) 319-9353

www.asylumdc.com

Asylum features industrial/ metal music, cheap beer, great burgers and fries.

Bar Nun

1326 U St., NW

(202) 667-6680

www.dcbarnun.com

Bar None offers Ethiopian food, performance art and poetry, hip-hop, jazz, and a large dance floor. Open every day of the week.

Brickskeller Saloon

1523 22 St., NW

(202) 293-1885

www.thebrickskeller.net

The Brick offers over 1,000 varieties of beer—more than any other bar in the world.

Hawk and Dove

329 Pennsylvania Ave., SE

(202) 543-3300

www.hawkanddoveonline.com

Attracts Capitol Hill staffers and military types; H&D has six rooms, a dance floor, and late-night breakfast and food specials.

Heaven and Hell

2327 18 St. NW

(202) 667-4355

A popular college dance spot, Heaven has an '80's night and techno music, and Hell has a more low-key bar scene with theme drinks like the red-hot 666 shot.

The Improv

1140 Connecticut Ave, NW

(202) 296-7008

www.dcimprov.com

The Improv has stand-up comedy acts that attract big name stars to perform— popular with college students and young people, with lots of good appetizers and a two-drink minimum.

MCCXXIII

1223 Connecticut Ave. NW

(202) 822-1800

Open Tuesday–Saturday, with a strict dress code: no sneakers, athletic gear, or hats. Drink specials nightly, including an open bar for $15 Thursday–Friday nights. Music includes hip hop, R&B, and house.

Madam's Organ

2461 18 St, NW

(202) 667-5370

www.madamsorgan.com

One of Adams Morgan's most popular bars, Madam's serves cheap drinks, food, pool tables, a hip, laid-back attitude, and has live music seven nights a week.

Marx Café

3203 Mount Pleasant St., NW

(202) 518-7600

This spot attracts young hipsters with its communist décor, reggae, Spanish rock music, and great tapas.

Recessions

1823 L St., NW

(202) 296-6686

www.recessionslounge.com

Recessions is a very cheap downtown bar in the basement of the Commerce building—a great after-work spot. Features nightly drink specials, and cheap food.

Zanzibar

700 Water St., SW

(202) 554-9100

www.zanzibar-otw.com

This is a glamorous bar on DC's waterfront, with exotic food and drinks (African and Caribbean). Zanz also has the best views of the Potomac River—three levels, two VIP lounges, and two sprawling outdoor decks.

Other Places to Check Out:

9:30 Nightclub

18th Street Lounge

Barking Dog

Black Cat

Bravo

Front Page

Malt Shoppe

Mouse Trap

Nanny O'Brien's

Prince's

Round Table

The Zoo

Bars Close At:

2 a.m.

Primary Areas with Nightlife:

Adams Morgan

Southeast DC

U Street

Cheapest Place to Get a Drink:

Recessions

Favorite Drinking Games:

Beer Pong

Card Games (A$$hole)

Century Club

Quarters

Power Hour

Student Favorites:

Hawk and Dove

Nation

Platinum

Useful Resources for Nightlife:

www.dcnightlife.com

What to Do if You're Not 21:

The Kennedy Center has cultural events like National Symphony performances.

Students Speak Out On...
Nightlife

"Some of the clubs are MCCXXIII, Dream, Nation, and Insomnia. Bars are a different story. There are countless numbers of bars here. Just take a bus downtown or to Georgetown, and you will find enough bars to drink yourself into oblivion."

Q "**Number one on the list is the 18th Street Lounge**. They don't advertise and there's no sign on the door, so you'll have to find someone to take you there. They actually own a record label, and there's usually live music some evenings. It's one of the hottest spots, in my estimation. It's also in the Dupont Circle area, near several other interesting places."

Q "There's an incredible range of bars and clubs, so everyone can find something they like. **Some places are all college students, and some have slightly older crowds**. Most clubs let you in if you're 18 and just card for drinking. Bars are similar. You can find bars that are known for serving kids who are underage, things like little college dive bars. Also try Irish pubs (my favorite is Nanny O'Brien's) and German bars."

Q "**Many of the incoming freshmen like to go to Platinum and Polly Esther's for dancing**. Places can be pricey, but I can vouch for Nation being a lot of fun, rave-style. If you like Latin dancing, there's Bravo—they have a great crowd and a low cover. Adams Morgan, another neighborhood, is a great place to party, but it's costly. It's a more uptight scene. There's little to do without an ID, although some of the clubs let women in if they are 18-and-up. For guys, it's only 21-and-up."

Q "DC has **so many amazing options** for nightlife. People go out clubbing every Tuesday, Thursday, Friday, and Saturday night. My fraternity has parties every week and smaller drinking get-togethers a few times a week."

Q "I'm more of a club person than a bar person, though it all depends on how good your ID is to get into the bars. **They are a bit strict in DC about IDs, so getting into bars is harder**. Nevertheless, there are some good ones in Georgetown. The clubs are really good, I would suggest MCCXXIII, which is like a bar lounge/club—it's on the more expensive side, but it's worth it. Platinum is also really fun."

Q "**Bars are fun, but absolutely notorious for carding**. But girls tend to have an easier time. You best get yourself a fake ID if you want to enjoy bars in DC."

Q "**DC is a great city for college kids and 20-somethings**, so there is always somewhere fun to go. Most of the clubs are '18 to get in, 21 to drink.' Don't try using a fake; they're really strict. My favorite ones are Daedalus, Platinum, and the Zoo, but the clubs are always changing names and styles of music, so it's fun to try new ones often. The bar named Recessions is shady, but it is all you can drink for $15 before midnight and everyone gets served. My favorite place is Front Page. It is known as a soccer team hangout, and I also like Barking Dog—a lot of frats rent it out and throw parties."

Q "**You can find places to go for anything you are into**. There are nice places, and there are ghetto places. However, one thing they all have in common is that the drinks are expensive. Drinks can cost as much as seven or eight bucks for like a Long Island Iced Tea. Beers could get up to $5. The bar and club scene, as opposed to the Greek scene, is pretty much the more popular choice on campus. Everyone at AU goes out on Tuesday night in addition to the weekend."

Q "Bars around school include the Malt Shoppe, and the Round Table, which has live music every weekend. Even though they are both kind of dives, they are banging on the weekends and filled with college kids. It's a great time. Further away, there are clubs like Daedalus, Nation, Platinum, and the 9:30 Nightclub. **If you like dancing, DC's got you covered.**"

Q "**Most cats at AU don't seem to be very interested in the local music scene.** But that doesn't mean there's not a variety of things to do in DC. I like going to Prince's in Georgetown to smoke shisha, dancing like an idiot at Mouse Trap, feeling out of place in various trance-oriented nightclubs downtown . . . you know, keeping it real."

Q "There are **no parties on campus**, since frats are not allowed on campus. However, there are parties, but they usually get busted. Bars and clubs are huge around all of DC, especially Adams Morgan and Dupont Circle."

The College Prowler Take On...
Nightlife

DC nightlife is active and exciting enough to wear the most energetic students out. Students will never run out of places to explore when it comes to clubbing and bar hopping. The most interesting places require only a short Metro ride, though there are some spots in Tenleytown for AU students. Clubs will usually admit 18-year-olds, but IDs are carefully checked.

Those who aren't big on dancing and drinking can keep themselves amused, too. Movie theaters, comedy clubs, shows, and concerts abound, as do restaurants and coffeehouses. You won't go bored here.

The College Prowler® Grade on
Nightlife: A-

A high grade in Nightlife indicates that there are many bars and clubs in the area that are easily accessible and affordable. Other determining factors include the number of options for the under-21 crowd and the prevalence of house parties.

Greek Life

The Lowdown On...
Greek Life

Number of Fraternities:
10, 1 colony

Number of Sororities:
13

Undergrad Men in Fraternities:
16%

Undergrad Women in Sororities:
17%

Fraternities on Campus:

Alpha Epsilon Pi
Alpha Sigma Phi
Delta Chi
Delta Tau Delta
Kappa Alpha Psi
Lambda Upsilon Lambda
Phi Beta Sigma
Phi Sigma Kappa
Pi Kappa Alpha
Pi Kappa Phi (Colony)
Sigma Chi

Sororities on Campus:

Alpha Chi Omega
Alpha Epsilon Phi
Alpha Kappa Alpha
Alpha Nu Omega
Chi Omega
Delta Gamma
Delta Sigma Theta
Lambda Pi Chi
Phi Mu
Phi Sigma Sigma
Sigma Delta Tau
Sigma Gamma Rho
Zeta Phi Beta

Other Greek Organizations:

Greek Council
Greek Peer Advisors
Interfraternity Council
Order of Omega
Panhellenic Council

Students Speak Out On...
Greek Life

"Greek life isn't a big deal. There are frats and sororities, but they definitely don't dominate the social scene. It's one of those things where you can definitely join if you want, but there isn't any pressure."

Q "There is a plethora of Greek organizations, from the typical beer frats to the do-good types. **They only dominate the school during rush week and Greek week**."

Q "**We have a pretty large Greek life on campus**, but it all depends where you live. If you live on the north side, Greek life isn't very popular, but on the south side, it pretty much dominates the dorm and social scene. Go for whichever you prefer. I really like that you have that option here at American."

Q "Last semester, I pledged a fraternity, and it opened up so many new options for my social life. **The Greek system doesn't dominate the social scene**, but joining a sorority or fraternity is almost always a great experience. There are groups for every kind of person, and most don't fit the typical Greek stereotype. Plus, there are great parties, mixers, formals, sporting events, and other functions only available to the Greek students."

Q "It absolutely does not dominate. That's one of the reasons that I came to this school. **There is Greek life and there are parties with free beer**, but if you are not in a frat or sorority, you're not the outcast of the AU social life. On the other hand, if you do want to get into it, that too is very easy. They pledge every fall and spring."

Q "Greek life does not dominate the social scene but it's big enough. There is something like 10 fraternities, and 13 sororities. **Each frat is pretty different**. You have your good ones, your dorky ones, your meatheads, and your hotshots. I personally think it's a well-rounded system."

Q "I'm in a frat and it is fun, but honestly, the sororities are bigger. **Since we are a dry campus, it kind of takes away from the Greek experience**. Since then, Greek life is still around but it's not as prevalent. We throw parties a lot, but when they get too big, they get broken up by cops."

Q "The Greeks seem to exist only to lend a more collegiate air to the campus, like cuff links round out the sleeves of a dress shirt. **Greeks do not dominate the social scene; they exist because of it**."

Q "**Who cares**?"

Q "There are a couple frats that don't **drop roofies** in your drinks."

Q "About **20 percent of AU is Greek** . . . it's really not a big deal at all. You can make friends easily here whether you are Greek or not."

The College Prowler Take On...
Greek Life

Students interested in Greek life have plenty of options as to which fraternities and sororities to join, although there are no houses for them on campus. Frats and sororities are a good choice for people who feel overwhelmed and want a surefire way to make friends. Students who don't care about Greek life need not worry, as it is entirely possible to ignore.

Many of the students involved in Greek life live on the noisier south side of campus and are responsible for the rowdy environment there. This makes them easily recognizable for anyone who wants to join in their activities—or anyone who wishes to avoid them like the plague.

The College Prowler® Grade on
Greek Life: B

A high grade in Greek Life indicates that sororities and fraternities are not only present, but also active on campus. Other determining factors include the variety of houses available and the respect the Greek community receives from the rest of the campus.

Drug Scene

The Lowdown On...
Drug Scene

Most Prevalent Drugs on Campus:
Alcohol
Ecstasy
Marijuana

Liquor-Related Referrals:
237

Liquor-Related Arrests:
0

Drug-Related Referrals:
66

Drug-Related Arrests:
0

Drug Counseling Programs

AU's Health Center provides information about drug and alcohol abuse as well as one-on-one counseling services. They can also put students in touch with clinics and support groups such as AA and NA contact info.

The Counseling Center offers both single-session "Being Your Best" workshops and ongoing support groups every semester, and these usually include sessions of interest to students concerned about their drug/alcohol use. There are also many support groups in the DC area sponsored by various national "12-step" programs, including S.M.A.R.T, Smart Recovery, Alcohol Anonymous (AA), Adult Children of Alcoholics (ACOA), Al-Anon, Narcotics Anonymous (NA), and Cocaine Anonymous (CA).

Students Speak Out On...
Drug Scene

{ **"There's a drug scene, which I was mostly oblivious to. There were a couple of students who were known dealers, but it was something that we mostly ignored. Lots of people drink and do pot."**

Q "I can't comment personally, except to say **it's available**."

Q "If you know the right people, you can definitely find drugs. **Alcohol is easy to come by**, so there isn't a problem there. If you wanted to, you could pretty much find weed anytime."

Q "**Drugs are there pretty much if you want them**. As long as you aren't stupid about it, nobody really cares. People do talk, and if you smoke like 20 pounds of weed an hour, people will start talking about how you now have the IQ of a green onion. But truthfully, if you want it, it is there for the taking and if not, it isn't there."

Q "There is lots of weed and some people are into crystal meth, but **you really don't see it unless you're looking for it**."

Q "**Pot is probably the most heavily-used drug**, but even that is not all that prevalent. I've heard of other things being used—acid, E, and coke—but I've never actually seen anyone use them. If you don't want to do drugs, you don't have to. Don't try stuff on campus; they are strict about it. Drinking is this school's stronghold."

Q "**Drugs are there but not too prevalent**. I don't see them much, but if you want them, they're there."

Q "I have to say, the drug scene is pretty big. We had a huge bust a while back, and the police found about five pounds of weed and $15,000 in drug money. **A lot of people smoke, and some do harder drugs, too**. If you're into that scene, it's definitely around. If not, you can avoid it, too."

Q "**It's a college full of rich kids who have no worries**. That means you have your cocaine, pot, some opium, and maybe some 'shrooms. Despite that, it's not huge, but it's present."

Q "**Our campus is very strict**. There is no drinking or pot (obviously) allowed on campus. If you get caught, you must do community service. If you get caught a second time, you have to do even more community service and also go to an educational mediation session. The best bet is to go off campus for that. People still get away with it on campus, but you just have to be careful and smart."

Q "**Our last major drug bust, years back, was covered by television news**, the *Washington Post*, and *Rolling Stone*. Make of that what you will."

Q "**The drug scene exists**, but is not destructive to those who want nothing to do with it."

Q "**There is so much to do in the city and on campus** . . . there are other things to occupy your time."

The College Prowler Take On...
Drug Scene

Though students say there is a large variety of drugs available on campus, ranging from pot to opium, it is easy to avoid them. Drugs are not an intricate part of students' social life at AU, but for those that want them, they are certainly there.

AU is known to be a strict campus that has recently cracked down on the drug scene by confiscating drugs and severely punishing the student drug dealers involved. Despite its presence, it's quite possible to not even see one drug during your entire four years of college at AU. So, don't let that deter you from coming here.

The College Prowler® Grade on

Drug Scene: A-

A high grade in the Drug Scene indicates that drugs are not a noticeable part of campus life; drug use is not visible, and no pressure to use them seems to exist.

Campus Strictness

The Lowdown On...
Campus Strictness

What Are You Most Likely to Get Caught Doing on Campus?

- Drinking
- Smoking weed
- Violating quiet hour rules

Students Speak Out On...
Campus Strictness

"It is a dry campus. The only place you can have alcohol is in the tavern, and you have to obviously be 21 and drink it there. No one really cares though, if you aren't loud about it."

Q "If they catch you, I think they're pretty strict, but if you're sitting in your room drinking and not making a ton of noise, you generally won't get caught."

Q "For the record, AU is a dry campus. It is pretty lenient on drinking, unless you make an idiot of yourself doing it. Don't get caught—it's easy not to get caught. Drugs are trickier. They exist as much as they do on any campus, but we don't have a huge problem because most people are here to study and take advantage of the city. If you're looking for a more lenient place in that area, this probably wouldn't be your best bet."

Q "AU is 'technically' a dry campus, meaning no alcohol, even if you're 21. The reality is, people drink in the dorms all the time, and it's just the ones who are stupid about it that get caught. There's definitely a drug scene that ranges from pot to some hardcore drug dealing, but most of it gets ignored."

Q "The campus is as strict as it can be without acting like our parents."

Q "If you roll a keg into the elevator, that is bad. People will bust you. **Just be quiet, and everything will work out**. It is the same with the drug scene. We had a big drug bust here a few years ago but that was completely because the kids were stupid about it."

Q "Public safety is pretty strict. It depends on your resident assistant (RA) most of the time. **Freshman year, my RA sucked, but we still drank in our rooms**. We were just careful. Last year, my RA didn't care at all. If you get caught, you have to go to meetings for about a week."

Q "It **totally depends on your RA**. If they are strict and get you in trouble, then you will be subject to the University's strict rules. If they are lax, then you don't have to worry as much about getting into trouble."

Q "The campus police are very strict, especially since we have a dry campus. **Not even 21-year-olds are allowed to have alcohol on campus**. You can be drunk on campus, but you cannot be drinking."

Q "Campus police are not particularly strict. It's a dry campus, but it's **not difficult to get around** that."

Q "It depends on the dorm, but **if you get caught, chances are something will happen to you**, depending on how many previous offenses are on your record."

The College Prowler Take On...
Campus Strictness

The trick to being wild and crazy at AU is to do it quietly. Being an enclosed campus, there is not much that students can get away with without campus security noticing. Also, because they have the right to turn you into campus police for punishment, who you get as an RA can decidedly determine your fate.

Students believe that their campus upholds strict rules and penalties when it comes to keeping everyone in line, and as a dry campus, alcohol is not permitted anywhere on the school grounds, even for those over 21. Several students mention recent drug busts, so be forewarned that the campus is cracking down on any and all illegal activity. The advice from current students: if you must partake in activities that the school forbids, then do it quietly in your room and, odds are, you won't get in trouble.

The College Prowler® Grade on

Campus Strictness: D

A high Campus Strictness grade implies an overall lenient atmosphere; police and RAs are fairly tolerant, and the administration's rules are flexible.

Parking

The Lowdown On...
Parking

Approximate Parking Permit Cost:

$880/year for on-campus students

$880/year for full-time commuting students

$335/year for motorcyclists

$335/year for part-time commuting students

AU Parking Services:

Contact through Transportation Services at (202) 885-3111.

www.american.edu/finance/ts/index.html

Student Parking Lot?

Yes

Freshmen Allowed to Park?

No

Parking Permits:

Purchase through Public Safety

→

Common Parking Tickets:

$10 fine: Failure to properly display current AU parking permit.

$30 fine: Unauthorized Parking—parking with or without a permit in the wrong lot/parking area or in a designated reserved parking space, service vehicle space, or loading zone without the proper permit.

$40 fine: Absence of current permit meter violation—parking at an expired or broken meter.

$75 fine: Parking in Neighborhood Areas—parking on neighborhood streets adjacent to campus.

$60 fine: No Parking Area—parking with or without a permit in a posted no parking area. Impeding Traffic—unauthorized parking or stopping your vehicle on a University roadway, pedestrian crosswalk, or intersection.

Boot Fee—fee assessed for booted vehicles with three unpaid tickets or falsified permits.

$150 fine: Handicap Parking—parking in a designated handicap parking space without the required handicap license tag or handicap parking permit. This violation also is issued to vehicles blocking curb cuts and handicap access ramps.

Did You Know?

Best Places to Find a Parking Spot
Nebraska parking lot, parking garage, side streets

Good Luck Getting a Parking Spot Here!
The lots behind the dorms

Students Speak Out On...
Parking

"Parking is pretty non existent on campus for students. You can't have a car on campus when you are a freshman, and getting on-campus parking permits is hard and expensive."

Q "You have to have a parking permit to park on campus. **Most people don't have cars, and in DC you really don't need one**. My roommate had a car part of the time, and when we lived on campus with the car, it wasn't a problem to get a permit. When we lived off campus, we would only drive to campus at night after some of the parking restrictions were lifted. It's a self-contained campus with really only one road going through, so it's not like there's 'on-street' parking on campus. There is only some parking around the campus."

Q "Let me be very clear—you don't need a car here until you live off campus. **Parking on campus can be arranged (for an exorbitant fee), but parking in the city is a nightmare**. There is a free shuttle from campus to the Metro station every 15 minutes to half-an-hour, and cabs go wherever you want after the Metro closes. Cabs are expensive—Metro is not."

Q "**Parking is very expensive in DC** and could cost you upwards of $130 a month. I would suggest you don't bring a car. DC has one of the best public transportation systems in the country. You won't really need a car anyway. There are a lot of bars and restaurants within walking distance, and the heart of DC is just a five-minute train ride away."

Q "**Parking is expensive**, but if you buy a permit, there are lots of spots."

Q "Parking sucks. **If you bring your car, you need to apply for a permit way in advance**. You can't park on campus without one. Take it from me; I have paid over $1,000 in fines since I've been here. Your best bet is to just leave your car home. There really is no reason to have a car here."

Q "**Don't bring a car**. It's expensive and really hard to find parking. Plus, there is really no point, because public transportation is really good in DC and really safe. You can also walk to a lot of places from campus."

Q "Parking is expensive on campus, but **if you buy a permit, it's easy to park**. Campus is really small, so it's easy to get around. I didn't have a car for my first two and a half years, and I got around DC fine."

Q "**Don't bring a car to live on campus** unless you hate yourself."

Q "It may be easy to park, but it's not easy to pay for it. **A car is redundant in DC anyway**."

Q "It sucks to park. It's expensive, and if you park on a public street outside AU, you can still get a ticket from AU if you don't have an AU permit. Of course, **cars aren't usually needed for most students**."

The College Prowler Take On...
Parking

Parking in DC and on the AU campus is an expensive hassle. AU doesn't allow first-year students to bring cars to campus, and street parking is difficult to find because of the exclusive nature of the surrounding residential area. Parking permits are expensive, running about $450 a semester, and students need to apply for them way in advance. However, if students do get a permit, they believe it is fairly easy to find a spot in one of the on-campus lots.

Students often walk to nearby bars and restaurants and need cars only if they move off campus. Even then, many use the accessible Metro and take the shuttle back and forth from campus. Basically, because DC offers such extensive and inexpensive public transportation, bringing your own car is pretty unnecessary.

D-

The College Prowler® Grade on

Parking: D-

A high grade in this section indicates that parking is both available and affordable, and that parking enforcement isn't overly severe.

Transportation

The Lowdown On...
Transportation

Ways to Get Around Town:

On Campus
AU shuttles and on foot

Public Transportation
AU shuttles, buses, and the Metro

The Metro
(202) 637-7000
www.wmata.com

Taxi Cabs
Diamond Cab DC
110 Q St., NW
(202) 387-6200

Empire Cab
1625 S. Capitol St., SW
(202) 488-4844

Lincoln Cab
129 Q St., SW
(202) 484-2222

Mayflower Cab
920 1st St., SE
(202) 783-1111

Yellow Cab
1636 Bladensburg Rd., NE
(202) 544-1212

→

Car Rentals

Alamo
national: (800) 327-9633
www.alamo.com

Avis
national: (800) 831-2847
www.avis.com

Budget
national: (800) 527-0700
www.budget.com

Dollar
national: (800) 800-4000
www.dollar.com

Enterprise
national: (800) 736-8222
www.enterprise.com

Hertz
national: (800) 654-3131
www.hertz.com

National
national: (800) 227-7368
www.nationalcar.com

Best Ways to Get Around Town

Metro!

Ways to Get Out of Town:

Amtrak, Greyhound, MARC, commuter rail, planes from Reagan National, Dulles, and BWI airports

Airlines Serving DC

AirTran
(800) AIR-TRAN
www.airtran.com

Alaska Airlines
(800) 252-7522
www.alaskaair.com

America West
(800) 235-9292
www.americawest.com

American
(800) 433-7300
www.aa.com

American Trans Air
(800) 225-2995
www.ata.com

British Airways
(800) 247-9297
www.british-airways.com

Continental
(800) 525-0280
www.continental.com

Delta
(800) 221-1212
www.delta.com

Frontier
(800) 432-1359
www.frontierairlines.com

Jet Blue
(800) 538-2583
www.jetblue.com

Midwest Express
(800) 452-2022
www.midwestexpress.com

Northwest
(800) 225-2525
www.nwa.com

Southwest
(800) 435-9792
www.southwest.com

**(Airlines Serving
DC, continued)**

Spirit
(800) 772-7117
www.spiritair.com

US Airways
(800) 428-4322
www.usairways.com

A cab ride to the airport costs
between $18–$25.

Greyhound
1005 1st St., NE
(202) 289-5154
www.greyhound.com

Amtrak
900 2nd St., NE
(202) 906-2199
www.amtrak.com

Both available from
Union Station.

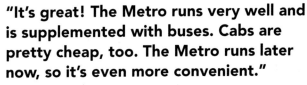

Students Speak Out On...
Transportation

> "It's great! The Metro runs very well and is supplemented with buses. Cabs are pretty cheap, too. The Metro runs later now, so it's even more convenient."

Q "**Transportation around DC is easy**. We are a short shuttle ride to the Metro stop, which is clean, safe, and will take you to practically any spot in DC."

Q "It's very convenient. **Public transportation is great** and arguably the easiest and most efficient in the country."

Q "Public transport is amazing in DC. We have the Metro subway, **the buses are pretty good**, and you can pretty much get a taxi anywhere."

Q "It is very convenient. There are buses, the Metro, and cabs that will take you everywhere you need. **Shuttles from campus take you to the closest Metro stop**."

Q "The Metro is awesome. I'm from New York, and the DC subway system easily beats it. It is so convenient. **It's the cleanest subway you will find in this country**."

Q "It is so convenient. You won't be disappointed. There is a **shuttle on campus that runs every 15 minutes** and brings you to the subway and major bus route."

Q "The Metro system is **the best transportation network in the history of the universe** and beyond . . ."

Q "**The Metro is the best**. It's easy, convenient, and clean. I approve.'"

Q "Public transportation is great. The AU shuttle takes you to the Metro and the city bus system. Of course, **you can always take a cab, but that's expensive**."

The College Prowler Take On...
Transportation

Hands down, DC is celebrated by students as one of the easiest cities to get around. The Metro, one of the cleanest and most efficient subway systems in the country, runs through DC and even into parts of Virginia and Maryland. Students at AU praise the Metro for its ease, convenience, and proximity to campus. They are able to visit other neighborhoods and get in, out, and around town both quickly and inexpensively.

The Tenleytown Metro stop is the closest to AU, and a short shuttle ride from campus to the stop links students with the entire DC area. With such an extensive Metro system, public transportation is definitely the preferred method of transportation among American University students.

The College Prowler® Grade on

Transportation: A

A high grade for Transportation indicates that campus buses, public buses, cabs, and rental cars are readily-available and affordable. Other determining factors include proximity to an airport and the necessity of transportation.

Weather

The Lowdown On...
Weather

Average Temperature:

Fall: 59°F
Winter: 34°F
Spring: 56°F
Summer: 79°F

Average Precipitation:

Fall: 3.10 in.
Winter: 2.83 in.
Spring: 3.36 in.
Summer: 3.80 in

Students Speak Out On...
Weather

{ **"The weather is very mild during winter. Sometimes we get snow, but not very much. Fall is long and beautiful, as is spring. August and September are usually quite warm and humid with temperatures in the 80s and 90s. It rains a lot in winter."**

Q "The glorious East Coast! We have humid summers, cold winters, and **fabulous falls and springs**."

Q "We usually get two or three snowfalls in the winter, and **the summers can get up to 90–100 degrees**. One thing I notice about the weather here is that it goes back and forth in the transition seasons. For example, a few weeks ago this spring, it was in the 90s for a few days. Last week, it was in the 50s and 60s. Today, it was 75. It jumps back and forth."

Q "The weather here is crazy. **Sometimes it is freezing and other days it is blistering hot**. Historically, DC used to shut down in the summer because it would get so hot. Also, I've heard that DC was built on a swamp, so it is very humid in the summer."

Q "For some reason this year, the weather has been really weird. There was a week when it got really hot, then it suddenly got cooler. But generally, **during the winter it's cold, and during the spring it gets warmer**. We get all four seasons here."

Q "The weather in DC is great. **It's nice when you can wear shorts in March**."

Q "**You probably won't see that much snow in the winter**. The DC area never gets hit that hard. I like avoiding the 20-degree winters that I was accustomed to before I came here. The temperatures are much milder. September and April are hot, though."

Q "Let's just say don't come here for the weather. It's humid in the fall and spring, and in the winter, it's cold, but not cold enough to really snow. **The only nice part is in the spring when the cherry blossoms bloom**; it's gorgeous."

Q "The weather is pretty good. It does snow in the winter, but not much. However, it can get **really humid from May through August**."

Q "**It's hot and muggy in the summer**. Snow doesn't come too often in winter, but in general, it's nice."

Q "**August is so muggy . . . prepare to sweat**. Winters are comparatively mild to western parts of the US. 3–4 inches of snow will get you a snow day."

Q "September through mid-October and late-March through May are gorgeous times. Everything in between is rain. DC, despite it's urban setting, has **the best sunsets of anywhere I've been**."

Q "**The weather is completely insane**: hot, hot, humid summers, lovely falls, unpredictable winters, and gorgeous (but also unpredictable) springs. Bring a wide variety of clothes (including an umbrella!)."

The College Prowler Take On...
Weather

DC weather tends to be slightly schizophrenic—hot, humid summers, cool winters with some snow, and springs that can range from warm and pleasant to monsoon-infested. AU students' reactions to the weather depend on what they're normally accustomed to, but most say they like the mild winters and long falls.

Students should bring a wide range of clothes for the varied climate. Umbrellas are a must. As long as you build up a tolerance for some rain and unpredictable weather, you should have no problem exploring the city and sightseeing.

The College Prowler® Grade on
Weather: B-

A high Weather grade designates that temperatures are mild and rarely reach extremes, that the campus tends to be sunny rather than rainy, and that weather is fairly consistent rather than unpredictable.

Report Card Summary

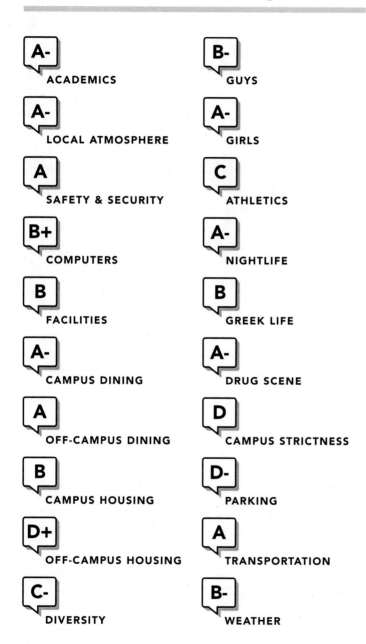

A- ACADEMICS

B- GUYS

A- LOCAL ATMOSPHERE

A- GIRLS

A SAFETY & SECURITY

C ATHLETICS

B+ COMPUTERS

A- NIGHTLIFE

B FACILITIES

B GREEK LIFE

A- CAMPUS DINING

A- DRUG SCENE

A OFF-CAMPUS DINING

D CAMPUS STRICTNESS

B CAMPUS HOUSING

D- PARKING

D+ OFF-CAMPUS HOUSING

A TRANSPORTATION

C- DIVERSITY

B- WEATHER

Overall Experience

Students Speak Out On...
Overall Experience

"I love this school. I wouldn't change it for the world. My brother is going to be a freshman in the fall, because he has seen how much I love AU and wants to come here, too!"

Q "I've had frustrations thanks to the bureaucracy that surrounds any such institution, but I'm happy I chose AU, and I would recommend it to anyone who cares about diversity, government, and high second-tier academics with more than a few shining stars. **It's quite possible to be very happy here**."

Q "**Sometimes I wish I went to a state school because the partying there is just ridiculous**. I have visited friends at state schools and have seen the madness that occurs. But truthfully, it just depends on what kind of place you're looking for. If you go to a state school, it will most likely have better parties, but you are just another face in the crowd. When you go to a party here, you see a lot of people you know, and I think I like that about AU. Plus, DC is a great city. There is always something going on. For the Fourth of July, we all go down to the National Mall and watch the most amazing fireworks show on earth."

Q "I have a better perspective of AU than I had coming in. **There are friendships started there that really last forever**. Much like Stanford and other private schools, many people come here and never leave."

Q "I really like it at AU. I came for two reasons—a journalism degree and the District of Columbia. Both desires were fulfilled, and I still managed to have fun. No matter where you come from, **DC manages to be a city that still feels like home**."

Q "I had a great experience at American. I certainly have my criticisms of the school, but **overall, I'm really glad I went there**. My academic experience was good, and even better was the education that I got from the people around me. They were smart, engaged in the world, interesting, and diverse. Living in DC was incredible, and I still miss it sometimes. I had a lot of good times there, and I recommend it to anyone."

Q "I wish I had studied more when I was there. **AU is kind of too easy**."

Q "AU is a small school, which some people like and some people don't. **Personally, I enjoy walking around campus**, seeing familiar faces, and then seeing those same familiar faces at bars and clubs. AU really is a small community inside of DC. Walking from your dorm to class, it is very easy to see your friends and people you know. This is usually a positive, but the downside is that gossip moves fast, and everybody seems to be connected through friends or somebody they know, especially inside the Greek system. Either way, that is something you get used to, and it can make the social life very interesting."

Q "I really like school so far. I have met some really cool people, and the academics have been good, too. **I wanted the small-campus environment** because I came from a small high school, and I like the close community feeling. I think it all depends on what you prefer."

Q "To be honest, I wish I were somewhere else. I'm graduating in December and can't wait to get out of here. I know lots of people who are happy at AU, but **I think I could have been much happier at a larger university**. However, I am happier now that I've changed my major."

Q "I love it here. I am graduating next spring, and these years flew by. I don't wish anything to be different. **I do wish I could go back to the beginning and do it all over again**. It was a blast."

Q "I really liked AU. **It's a beautiful campus** that doesn't even take 25 minutes to walk across like some big schools. There are so many opportunities in DC. The only reason I would switch schools is for a bigger sports scene, but that is not a true reason to pick a school."

Q "When I first came, I hated it and wanted to transfer. It was difficult for me to adjust to such a diverse population, and I had trouble finding people I could relate to. Also, the lack of sports really got to me. But after some time, I loosened up a little, met some new people, accepted the school for what it was, and had a blast. Second semester was amazing, I love everything about American—all it's little quirks and how much it has taught me about the world. Plus, DC is the best city ever. I would never trade my experience for any one of my friends' experiences **It has been, hands down, the best years of my life**. Go with an open mind, and you'll love it.

Q "I have enjoyed my experience here. It was the right choice for me. This will not be the case for everyone; **it's largely dependent on how comfortable you feel in a city** and the major you're in (biology majors—look elsewhere)."

Q "The overall experience from the school itself is good, but **the academic experience coupled with extracurriculars and city life** make the college experience at American University top notch. Sometimes, I wish I was a farmer in the Midwest or a royal in the British Isles, or a cabaret performer in France, or a postman in Hawaii, or a boat captain in the Indian Ocean, or a village god being worshipped in Zambia. But that has nothing to do with school."

Q "I wouldn't go anywhere else. Although there are things that bug me about AU, this school has what I want and need. **It's a great atmosphere with distinguished faculty, bright students**, and interesting politics."

The College Prowler Take On...
Overall Experience

Many AU students agree that there is something for everyone at their school, and they are rarely ever bored. Though the school's population is relatively small and has fewer parties compared to state schools, many claim that it is worth it for the culture present in DC and the surrounding area.

Upon arrival at AU, the adjustment period can be tough for people not accustomed to an urban setting. However, making friends is quite easy here for even the shyest of students because of the small, tight-knit AU community. Students here, for the most part, have no problems expressing themselves socially or academically. It seems that a "work hard, play hard" philosophy best suits the students at American University.

The Inside Scoop

The Lowdown On...
The Inside Scoop

AU Slang:

Know the slang, know the school. The following is a list of things you really need to know before coming to AU. The more of these words you know, the better off you'll be.

Benladner.com – A hilarious Web site about AU run by several of it's students, named after the school president.

Flaming Cupcake – The flame design protruding from the roof of the Kay Spiritual Center.

Floorcest – Hooking up with someone on your own floor.

Getting "IRFed" – Getting written up by your RA for various rule violations.

Once an Eagle, Always an Eagle – The slogan for AU alums, especially sports fans.

Sexile – To kick your roomate out so you can hook up.

TDR – Terrace Dining Room—the main cafeteria at AU.

The Vagina Room – A semi-private dining room in TDR featuring Georgia O'Keeffe paintings.

Things I Wish I Knew Before Coming to AU

- It's not as small as you think.
- It's harder to find a date than you think.
- Driving and parking can be hellish; use the Metro whenever you can.
- DC is an extremely varied and cultural city, and all four quadrants deserve exploring.
- If you're not up on current events, count on being left out of many conversations and discussions.
- Ambition, intelligence, and strong opinions are often valued over looks or background.

Tips to Succeed at AU

- Get involved in extracurriculars to meet people and get good resume experience.
- Read a newspaper every day. (They're free in the dorms.)
- Form relationships with your professors.
- Try not to fight with your floormates—you'll have to live with them all year.
- Get out into DC as much as possible!

AU Urban Legends

- An old woman who lived near campus donated a huge sum of money before her death for the perpetual garden maintenance that goes on.
- The black squirrels and gray squirrels that live on campus constantly fight each other.
- A giant mutant beaver-type creature prowls the campus at night.

School Spirit

The Screaming Eagles are a club that actively supports the sports teams (think customized T-shirts, face paint, and wild and crazy cheers).

Traditions

Around finals time, students gather in the courtyard between Hughes and McDowell Halls to yell their heads off for Primal Scream and watch other students flash them from the overlooking dorms. It's a stress reliever. . .

Finding a Job or Internship

The Lowdown On...
Finding a Job or Internship

The best way to snag a great job or internship is to hit up the campus career center. They offer such services as resume critiques, mock interviews, and their own site on *monster.com*. Their advisors tend to be very knowledgeable and helpful, and can hook up students with opportunities out in DC that are well suited to their majors and interests. Another option is to peruse the JobCorps listings at *www.studentconfederation. org/jobcorps*. There is so much available in the city that it would be difficult not to find something.

Advice

Make use of the career center. Learn how to write professional cover letters and resumes, and keep your eyes opened for fliers posted around campus offering positions. Surf the Internet for opportunities, and form relationships with your professors so they can write you recommendations or give you advice on where to apply.

Grads Who Enter the Job Market Within

6 Months: 74%
1 Year: 78%

Firms That Most Frequently Hire Grads

Clear Channel Radio, Deloitte and Touche LLP, International Center for Research on Women, National Institutes of Health, Peace Corps, Teach for America, U.S. Department of Justice, U.S. Department of State

Alumni

The Lowdown On...
Alumni

Web Site:
http://alumni.american.edu

Office:
Office of Development
American University
4400 Massachusetts Ave.,
NW
Washington, DC 20016-8143
(202) 885-5960
gift@american.edu

Services Available:
AU store discounts, alumni
career services, insurance,
national chapters

Major Alumni Events:
Homecomings, reunions,
travel opportunities

Alumni Publication:
Alumni Association
Newsletter

Did You Know?

Famous AU Alumni

Robert Byrd (Class of '63) – Senator (D-WV)

Judith Sheindlin "Judge Judy" (Class of '63) – TV show host

Al Koken (Class of '74) – Talkshow Host, WTEM Sports Talk Radio

Robert Engel (Class of '82) – Executive Director, Committee for an Effective Congress

Goldie Hawn (Incomplete degree) – Actress

Star Jones (Class of '83) – Co-host, *The View*

David Aldridge (Class of '87) – ESPN analyst

Mike Mills (Class of '88) – Staff Writer, the *Washington Post*

Student Organizations

Clubs are listed on the Student Confederation's Web site, *http://www.american.edu/ocl/activities/student_organizations/AUCC.html*. The most popular organizations on campus are:

Animal Rights Effort – To promote better living through animal-friendly eating.

Black Student Alliance – To serve as a representative organization for all students of African descent at AU.

College Republicans – To educate about and promote ideas consistent with those of the Republican Party.

Latino & American Student Organization (LASO) – To unite in the advancement and education of the Latino community.

Model United Nations Model U.N. – To compete nationally against other college and university UN teams practicing diplomacy and mock international affairs.

Queers and Allies – Social and political organization designed to both promote visibility and awareness of GLBTA issues on campus and in the community and to provide safe space for peoples of all sexual orientations at AU.

The following is a list of all AU campus organizations:

AMC/Kernel Panic
Adopt-A-Grandparent
Adoption Awareness
Advocates for the Millennium
African Student Organization
Alpha Phi Omega
Alternative Spring Break
American Marketing Association
American Medical Student Association of AU
Amnesty International of AU
Anime Society
Arab Student Association
Asia MBA Club
Asian Students Association
Astronomers
A-Team
Audio Engineering Society
Autonomous Feminist Action
Bahai Club
Barkada: The Philippine Society
Baptist Student Fellowship
Campaign to End the Death Penalty, AU
Campus Crusade for Christ
Caribbean Circle
Catholic Community Choir and Ensemble
Catholic Student Association
Chi Alpha Christian Fellowship

Chi and Chat
Chinese Students and Scholars Association
Choice USA, AU
Circle K
Club Bulgaria
College Democrats
College Libertarians
Comedic Writers' Association
Committee on the Present Danger
Concerned Black Men of AU
Concert Choir
Consulting Team, American University (ACT)
Debate Society
Democracy Matters: Money and Politics
Design Club
Dime A Dozen
Eco-Sense
Educators for Critical Literacy
English Literacy Project
Entrepreneurs Club
Episcopal Campus Ministries
Facilitating Leadership in Youth (FLY)
Fair Trade Student Association
Falun Dafa Club
Family Network, AU
Finance Group
Free Burma Coalition

French Club

Gamers

Generation Dean

Gentleman's Club

German Club

Gospel Choir

Gymnastics Club

Habitat For Humanity

Hip Hop Zone

Hispanic Club

Hunger and Homelessness Club

In Motion, AU

Independent Arts Collective

Intercultural Student Association

International Business Association

International Communication Student Forum

Int'l Development Program Student Association

InterVarsity Christian Fellowship

Investment Group

Jewish Student Association

Korean Bible Study

Korean Student Association

Liturgical Dance Ministry

Managing the Integration of Tech. and Business

Martial Arts Club

Math Club

Movement For Global Justice, The

Muslim Student Association

NAACP

Naked Truth, The (TNT)

National Conference on Organized Resistance

National Council for Negro Women

National Youth Rights Associaiton, AU (NYRA)

Native Tongue

Net Impact

On a Sensual Note

One Accord

Operation Noble Eagles

Outdoors Club, The

Persian American Society

Photography Club

Phi Alpha Delta Pre-law Fraternity

Ping Pong Club

Players, AU

Project Hope International

Project Sunshine

Public Relations Society of America

Real Estate Club

Red Cross Club of America

ReJoyce in Jesus Campus Fellowship

Reunite Pangea Society

Rude Mechanics AU's Shakespeare Troupe

Russian Club

Screaming Eagles

Scrimmage Soccer

Shining City Coalition

Sisters of the Yam

Society for Peace and Conflict Resolution

Society of Physics Students

Society of Professional Journalists

Solidarity Committee

South Asian Student Alliance (SASA)

Spanish Club

Speedy Eagles

Spellbound

Student Alumni Association

Student Movement for Internal Relief

Student Organization for African Studies

Student Pugwash USA

Students for Academic Freedom

Students for Clark

Students for John Kerry

Students for Israel

Students for Justice in Palestine

Students for Life

Symphony Orchestra Club

Taiwanese Student Association

Team AU – the AIDS Marathoners Club

Team Runn'g Heads

Tolkien Society, AU

Transfer Transitions

Treble in Paradise

Unitarian Universalists

United Methodist Student Association

Washington Youth Partnership

Women in Business

Yoga Collective

Youth and Government

The Best & Worst

The Ten **BEST** Things About AU

1	Small classes
2	Friendly dorms
3	The world capitals program (for study abroad)
4	Exciting urban environment
5	Career center offering great job/internship opportunities
6	Large international student population
7	Good food on campus
8	Small campus makes it easy to get to class
9	Intelligent, activist student body
10	Expert professors

The Ten **WORST** Things About Au

1	The AU administration's favoritism toward the SPA and SIS
2	Weak biology department
3	Not much school spirit
4	The intense political environment can be overwhelming
5	Not much of a focus on the arts
6	High tuition
7	Expensive living conditions
8	Unbalanced female to male ratio
9	Not enough classes to choose from in certain departments
10	Students can be cliquish

Visiting

The Lowdown On...
Visiting

Hotel Information:

Bethesda Court Row
7740 Wisconsin Ave., NW
(301) 656-2100
Distance from Campus:
1.79 miles
Price Range: $79–$162

Embassy Suites
4300 Military Rd., NW
(202) 362-9300
Distance from Campus:
1.91 miles
Price Range: $135–$179

Hilton Embassy Row
2015 Massachusetts Ave., NW
(202) 265-1600
Distance from Campus:
3.97 miles
Price Range: $219–$264

Holiday Inn Chevy Chase
5520 Wisconsin Ave., NW
(301) 656-1500
Distance from Campus:
1.79 miles
Price Range: $167–$199

Holiday Inn Georgetown
2101 Wisconsin Ave. NW
(202) 338-4600
Distance from Campus:
2.88 miles
Price Range: $189–$228

Take a Campus Virtual Tour

www.american.edu/tour

To Schedule a Group Information Session or Interview

Contact the tours and information offices at (202) 885-6000 or e-mail afa@american.edu

Campus Tours

Visit AU's Web site for dates and times of tours and information sessions, or if you have any questions, please call admissions at (202) 885-6000.

Overnight Visits

Regular overnights, and special Honors overnights available. Orientations required for all incoming freshman in the summer. Separate orientation for international students.

Directions to Campus

From northeast of Washington
(New York, Philadelphia, Baltimore)
Follow Interstate 95 south to Interstate 495 west toward Silver Spring. See from Interstate 495 (Capital Beltway).

From south or west of Washington
(Norfolk, Richmond, Charlottsville)
Follow Interstate 95 north or Interstate 66 east to Interstate 495, the Capital Beltway. Follow Interstate 495 north. See from Interstate 495 (Capital Beltway).

From northwest of Washington
(Western Pennsylvania, Western Maryland)
Follow Interstate 270 south. Where Interstate 270 divides, follow the right-hand branch toward northern Virginia (not towards Washington). Merge with Interstate 495, the Capital Beltway, and soon afterwards take exit 39, River Road. See from Interstate 495 (Capital Beltway).

From Interstate 495 (Capital Beltway)
Take exit 39 and carefully follow the signs for River Road (Maryland Route 190) east toward Washington. Continue east on River Road to the fifth traffic light. Turn right onto Goldsboro Road (Maryland Route 614). At the first traffic light, turn left onto Massachusetts Avenue (Maryland Route 396). Continue on Massachusetts Avenue for about two miles, through the first traffic circle (Westmoreland Circle). About on mile further on, enter a second traffic circle (Ward Circle). Take the first right turn out of the circle, onto Nebraska Avenue. The campus is on your right.

From Nebraska Avenue
You may enter the University's visitor parking lot by turning left at the first traffic light onto New Mexico Avenue and then left into the parking lot adjacent to the Metropolitan Memorial United Methodist Church. Or you may drive directly onto the campus by driving past the first traffic light on Nebraska Avenue and turning right at the first gate. Very shortly, you will see a campus map on the right. It will direct you to The Admissions Welcome Center, located in Centennial Hall.

Words to Know

Academic Probation – A suspension imposed on a student if he or she fails to keep up with the school's minimum academic requirements. Those unable to improve their grades after receiving this warning can face dismissal.

Beer Pong/Beirut – A drinking game involving cups of beer arranged in a pyramid shape on each side of a table. The goal is to get a ping pong ball into one of the opponent's cups by throwing the ball or hitting it with a paddle. If the ball lands in a cup, the opponent is required to drink the beer.

Bid – An invitation from a fraternity or sorority to 'pledge' (join) that specific house.

Blue-Light Phone – Brightly-colored phone posts with a blue light bulb on top. These phones exist for security purposes and are located at various outside locations around most campuses. In an emergency, a student can pick up one of these phones (free of charge) to connect with campus police or a security escort.

Campus Police – Police who are specifically assigned to a given institution. Campus police are typically not regular city officers; they are employed by the university in a full-time capacity.

Club Sports – A level of sports that falls somewhere between varsity and intramural. If a student is unable to commit to a varsity team but has a lot of passion for athletics, a club sport could be a better, less intense option. Even less demanding, intramural (IM) sports often involve no traveling and considerably less time.

Cocaine – An illegal drug. Also known as "coke" or "blow," cocaine often resembles a white crystalline or powdery substance. It is highly addictive and dangerous.

Common Application – An application with which students can apply to multiple schools.

Course Registration – The period of official class selection for the upcoming quarter or semester. Prior to registration, it is best to prepare several back-up courses in case a particular class becomes full. If a course is full, students can place themselves on the waitlist, although this still does not guarantee entry.

Division Athletics – Athletic classifications range from Division I to Division III. Division IA is the most competitive, while Division III is considered to be the least competitive.

Dorm – A dorm (or dormitory) is an on-campus housing facility. Dorms can provide a range of options from suite-style rooms to more communal options that include shared bathrooms. Most first-year students live in dorms. Some upperclassmen who wish to stay on campus also choose this option.

Early Action – An application option with which a student can apply to a school and receive an early acceptance response without a binding commitment. This system is becoming less and less available.

Early Decision – An application option that students should use only if they are certain they plan to attend the school in question. If a student applies using the early decision option and is admitted, he or she is required and bound to attend that university. Admission rates are usually higher among students who apply through early decision, as the student is clearly indicating that the school is his or her first choice.

Ecstasy – An illegal drug. Also known as "E" or "X," ecstasy looks like a pill and most resembles an aspirin. Considered a party drug, ecstasy is very dangerous and can be deadly.

Ethernet – An extremely fast Internet connection available in most university-owned residence halls. To use an Ethernet connection properly, a student will need a network card and cable for his or her computer.

Fake ID – A counterfeit identification card that contains false information. Most commonly, students get fake IDs with altered birthdates so that they appear to be older than 21 (and therefore of legal drinking age). Even though it is illegal, many college students have fake IDs in hopes of purchasing alcohol or getting into bars.

Frosh – Slang for "freshman" or "freshmen."

Hazing – Initiation rituals administered by some fraternities or sororities as part of the pledging process. Many universities have outlawed hazing due to its degrading, and sometimes dangerous, nature.

Intramurals (IMs) – A popular, and usually free, sport league in which students create teams and compete against one another. These sports vary in competitiveness and can include a range of activities—everything from billiards to water polo. IM sports are a great way to meet people with similar interests.

Keg – Officially called a half-barrel, a keg contains roughly 200 12-ounce servings of beer.

LSD – An illegal drug, also known as acid, this hallucinogenic drug most commonly resembles a tab of paper.

Marijuana – An illegal drug, also known as weed or pot; along with alcohol, marijuana is one of the most commonly-found drugs on campuses across the country.

Major –The focal point of a student's college studies; a specific topic that is studied for a degree. Examples of majors include physics, English, history, computer science, economics, business, and music. Many students decide on a specific major before arriving on campus, while others are simply "undecided" until declaring a major. Those who are extremely interested in two areas can also choose to double major.

Meal Block – The equivalent of one meal. Students on a meal plan usually receive a fixed number of meals per week. Each meal, or "block," can be redeemed at the school's dining facilities in place of cash. Often, a student's weekly allotment of meal blocks will be forfeited if not used.

Minor – An additional focal point in a student's education. Often serving as a complement or addition to a student's main area of focus, a minor has fewer requirements and prerequisites to fulfill than a major. Minors are not required for graduation from most schools; however some students who want to explore many different interests choose to pursue both a major and a minor.

Mushrooms – An illegal drug. Also known as "'shrooms," this drug resembles regular mushrooms but is extremely hallucinogenic.

Off-Campus Housing – Housing from a particular landlord or rental group that is not affiliated with the university. Depending on the college, off-campus housing can range from extremely popular to non-existent. Students who choose to live off campus are typically given more freedom, but they also have to deal with possible subletting scenarios, furniture, bills, and other issues. In addition to these factors, rental prices and distance often affect a student's decision to move off campus.

Office Hours – Time that teachers set aside for students who have questions about coursework. Office hours are a good forum for students to go over any problems and to show interest in the subject material.

Pledging – The early phase of joining a fraternity or sorority, pledging takes place after a student has gone through rush and received a bid. Pledging usually lasts between one and two semesters. Once the pledging period is complete and a particular student has done everything that is required to become a member, that student is considered a brother or sister. If a fraternity or a sorority would decide to "haze" a group of students, this initiation would take place during the pledging period.

Private Institution – A school that does not use tax revenue to subsidize education costs. Private schools typically cost more than public schools and are usually smaller.

Prof – Slang for "professor."

Public Institution – A school that uses tax revenue to subsidize education costs. Public schools are often a good value for in-state residents and tend to be larger than most private colleges.

Quarter System (or Trimester System) – A type of academic calendar system. In this setup, students take classes for three academic periods. The first quarter usually starts in late September or early October and concludes right before Christmas. The second quarter usually starts around early to mid–January and finishes up around March or April. The last academic quarter, or "third quarter," usually starts in late March or early April and finishes up in late May or Mid-June. The fourth quarter is summer. The major difference between the quarter system and semester system is that students take more, less comprehensive courses under the quarter calendar.

RA (Resident Assistant) – A student leader who is assigned to a particular floor in a dormitory in order to help to the other students who live there. An RA's duties include ensuring student safety and providing assistance wherever possible.

Recitation – An extension of a specific course; a review session. Some classes, particularly large lectures, are supplemented with mandatory recitation sessions that provide a relatively personal class setting.

Rolling Admissions – A form of admissions. Most commonly found at public institutions, schools with this type of policy continue to accept students throughout the year until their class sizes are met. For example, some schools begin accepting students as early as December and will continue to do so until April or May.

Room and Board – This figure is typically the combined cost of a university-owned room and a meal plan.

Room Draw/Housing Lottery – A common way to pick on-campus room assignments for the following year. If a student decides to remain in university-owned housing, he or she is assigned a unique number that, along with seniority, is used to determine his or her housing for the next year.

Rush – The period in which students can meet the brothers and sisters of a particular chapter and find out if a given fraternity or sorority is right for them. Rushing a fraternity or a sorority is not a requirement at any school. The goal of rush is to give students who are serious about pledging a feel for what to expect.

Semester System – The most common type of academic calendar system at college campuses. This setup typically includes two semesters in a given school year. The fall semester starts around the end of August or early September and concludes before winter vacation. The spring semester usually starts in mid-January and ends in late April or May.

Student Center/Rec Center/Student Union – A common area on campus that often contains study areas, recreation facilities, and eateries. This building is often a good place to meet up with fellow students; depending on the school, the student center can have a huge role or a non-existent role in campus life.

Student ID – A university-issued photo ID that serves as a student's key to school-related functions. Some schools require students to show these cards in order to get into dorms, libraries, cafeterias, and other facilities. In addition to storing meal plan information, in some cases, a student ID can actually work as a debit card and allow students to purchase things from bookstores or local shops.

Suite – A type of dorm room. Unlike dorms that feature communal bathrooms shared by the entire floor, suites offer bathrooms shared only among the suite. Suite-style dorm rooms can house anywhere from two to ten students.

TA (Teacher's Assistant) – An undergraduate or grad student who helps in some manner with a specific course. In some cases, a TA will teach a class, assist a professor, grade assignments, or conduct office hours.

Undergraduate – A student in the process of studying for his or her bachelor's degree.

ABOUT THE AUTHOR

Writing this guidebook for College Prowler has been a great experience. I now know a lot more about American University and Washington, DC and can't wait to explore some new places. I'm currently a junior majoring in print journalism and Spanish, and I hope to continue writing. When at school, I write for *American Literary* and the *Eagle*, roam the clubs, hookah bars, movie theaters and museums of the city, and act like a weirdo with my floormates. I am originally from Long Island, NY, and moving from my suburban hometown to a school in one of the most exciting and powerful cities in the world has been incredible. I hope this book has been entertaining and informative for you, and that my enthusiasm for AU and DC is infectious!

Many thanks to: Mom, Dad, Julian, Nana, Omi and Opi, Erin, Lindsey, DZ, Anders, Kayley, Lini, Greg, Adrienne, Julia, MK, Josh, Shannon, Kalli, Nicole, Amanda, Aram, Megan, HC Crista, Crazy Cyrus, Ryan, The Jons, Spike, Dr. Romano, boomsauce, Andrew McCullough, Adam Burns, and all the folks at College Prowler.

Alanna Schubach
alannaschubach@collegeprowler.com

California Colleges

California dreamin'?

This book is a must have for you!

CALIFORNIA COLLEGES
7¼" X 10", 762 Pages Paperback
$29.95 Retail
1-59658-501-3

Stanford, UC Berkeley, Caltech—California is home to some of America's greatest institutes of higher learning. *California Colleges* gives the lowdown on 24 of the best, side by side, in one prodigious volume.

New England Colleges

Looking for peace in the Northeast?
Pick up this regional guide to New England!

NEW ENGLAND COLLEGES
7¼" X 10", 1015 Pages Paperback
$29.95 Retail
1-59658-504-8

New England is the birthplace of many prestigious
universities, and with so many to choose from, picking
the right school can be a tough decision. With inside
information on over 34 competive Northeastern
schools, *New England Colleges* provides the same
high-quality information prospective students expect
from College Prowler in one all-inclusive,
easy-to-use reference.

Schools of the South

Headin' down south? This book will help you find your way to the perfect school!

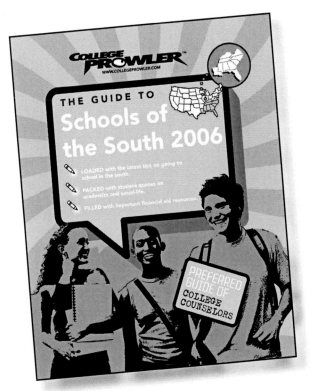

SCHOOLS OF THE SOUTH
7¼" X 10", 773 Pages Paperback
$29.95 Retail
1-59658-503-X

Southern pride is always strong. Whether it's across town or across state, many Southern students are devoted to their home sweet home. *Schools of the South* offers an honest student perspective on 36 universities available south of the Mason-Dixon.

Untangling
the Ivy League

The ultimate book for everything Ivy!

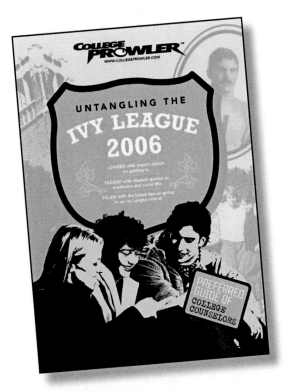

UNTANGLING THE IVY LEAGUE
7¼" X 10", 567 Pages Paperback
$24.95 Retail
1-59658-500-5

Ivy League students, alumni, admissions officers,
and other top insiders get together to tell it like it is.
Untangling the Ivy League covers every aspect—from
admissions and athletics to secret societies and urban
legends—of the nation's eight oldest, wealthiest, and
most competitive colleges and universities.

Need Help Paying For School?

Apply for our scholarship!

College Prowler awards thousands of dollars a year to students who compose the best essays. E-mail scholarship@collegeprowler.com for more information, or call 1-800-290-2682.

Apply now at ***www.collegeprowler.com***

Tell Us What Life Is Really Like at Your School!

Have you ever wanted to let people know what your college is really like? Now's your chance to help millions of high school students choose the right college.

Let your voice be heard.

Check out **www.collegeprowler.com** for more info!

Need More Help?

Do you have more questions about this school? Can't find a certain statistic? College Prowler is here to help. We are the best source of college information out there. We have a network of thousands of students who can get the latest information on any school to you ASAP. E-mail us at info@collegeprowler.com with your college-related questions.

E-Mail Us Your College-Related Questions!

Check out *www.collegeprowler.com* for more details.
1-800-290-2682

Write For Us!

Get published! Voice your opinion.

Writing a College Prowler guidebook is both fun and rewarding; our open-ended format allows your own creativity free reign. Our writers have been featured in national newspapers and have seen their names in bookstores across the country. Now is your chance to break into the publishing industry with one of the country's fastest-growing publishers!

Apply now at ***www.collegeprowler.com***

Contact editor@collegeprowler.com or
call 1-800-290-2682 for more details.

Pros and Cons

Still can't figure out if this is the right school for you?
You've already read through this in-depth guide; why not
list the pros and cons? It will really help with narrowing down
your decision and determining whether or not
this school is right for you.

Pros	Cons
....	....
....	....
....	....
....	....
....	....
....	....
....	....
....	....
....	....
....	....
....	....
....	....
....	....

Pros and Cons

Still can't figure out if this is the right school for you?
You've already read through this in-depth guide; why not
list the pros and cons? It will really help with narrowing down
your decision and determining whether or not
this school is right for you.

Pros	Cons
....	....
....	....
....	....
....	....
....	....
....	....
....	....
....	....
....	....
....	....
....	....
....	....
....	....

Notes

....

....

....

....

....

....

....

....

....

....

....

....

....

Notes

....

....

....

....

....

....

....

....

....

....

....

....

....

Notes

....

....

....

....

....

....

....

....

....

....

....

....

....

....

Notes

....

....

....

....

....

....

....

....

....

....

....

....

....

Notes

....

....

....

....

....

....

....

....

....

....

....

....

....

Notes

....

....

....

....

....

....

....

....

....

....

....

....

....

Notes

....
....
....
....
....
....
....
....
....
....
....
....
....
....

Notes

....

....

....

....

....

....

....

....

....

....

....

....

....

Notes

....

....

....

....

....

....

....

....

....

....

....

....

....

....

Notes

....

....

....

....

....

....

....

....

....

....

....

....

....

Notes

....
....
....
....
....
....
....
....
....
....
....
....
....

Notes

....

....

....

....

....

....

....

....

....

....

....

....

....

Notes

....

....

....

....

....

....

....

....

....

....

....

....

....

....

Notes

....

....

....

....

....

....

....

....

....

....

....

....

....

Notes

Notes

....

....

....

....

....

....

....

....

....

....

....

....

....

....

Notes

....

....

....

....

....

....

....

....

....

....

....

....

....

Notes

....

....

....

....

....

....

....

....

....

....

....

....

....

Notes

....

....

....

....

....

....

....

....

....

....

....

....

....

Notes

···

···

···

···

···

···

···

···

···

···

···

···

···

···

Notes

....

....

....

....

....

....

....

....

....

....

....

....

....

Notes

....

....

....

....

....

....

....

....

....

....

....

....

....

....

Notes

....

....

....

....

....

....

....

....

....

....

....

....

....

....

Notes

....

....

....

....

....

....

....

....

....

....

....

....

....

Notes

....
....
....
....
....
....
....
....
....
....
....
....
....

Notes

....

....

....

....

....

....

....

....

....

....

....

....

....

Notes

....

....

....

....

....

....

....

....

....

....

....

....

....